Vocabulary Power

GRADE 3

ISBN 0-15-320609-8

18 19 20 082 2009 2008 2007

Table of Contents

CHAPTER

CHAPTER

Name _____

RELATED WORDS

▶ There are many words that have to do with movies. Look at each category and write the words from the Word Box that best fit each group. Then add your own word to each group.

actors	cartoons	photographers
comedies	animated films	directors

WORKERS

KINDS OF
MOTION PICTURES

_____   _____

_____   _____

_____   _____

▶ Now try these.

lights	theater	on TV
film	cinema	camera

PLACES TO SEE MOVIES   MOVIE EQUIPMENT

_____   _____

_____   _____

_____   _____

Name _____

COMPARE AND CONTRAST

▶ **Look at each item. Then put a check in the box of each category that fits the item.**

		watched	heard	watched at a cinema	watched at home	characters can only be heard
1.	motion picture					
2.	television show					
3.	radio show					

▶ **Read and answer each question. Use complete sentences.**

4. What are some differences between a motion picture and a radio show?

_____

_____

_____

5. How are television shows and motion pictures alike?

_____

_____

Name _____

SYNONYMS

▶ Write each word from the Word Box next to its synonym. Then write an example for each pair of synonyms. The first one is done for you.

tune	motion picture	gem	theater	performer	cartoon

	Synonym	Example
1. movie	motion picture	*Black Beauty*
2. animated film	_____	_____
3. cinema	_____	_____
4. actor	_____	_____
5. song	_____	_____
6. jewel	_____	_____

▶ Now try these.

stream	town	car	creature	sea	street

7. automobile	_____	_____
8. road	_____	_____
9. river	_____	_____
10. ocean	_____	_____
11. city	_____	_____
12. animal	_____	_____

RELATED WORDS

Read each list of words. Think of how they are related. Circle the letter next to the correct topic. Then add a word of your own to each group of words.

I. flute, clarinet, oboe, _____
  A percussion instruments
  B tools
  C colors
  D woodwinds

2. fork, spoon, spatula, _____
  F music
  G utensils
  H foods
  J songs

3. drum, cymbal, tambourine, _____
  A percussion instruments
  B woodwinds
  C string instruments
  D horns

4. hammer, wrench, chisel, _____
  F shapes
  G percussion instruments
  H workers
  J devices

5. drummer, pianist, violinist, _____
  A woodwinds
  B percussion instruments
  C musicians
  D horns

Vocabulary Power

Name _____

ONOMATOPOEIA

Onomatopoeia words are words that imitate sounds.

Example: *clank, buzz*

▶ **Read each question and illustrate your answer.**

1. What kind of percussion instrument might make sounds like *boom* and *wham*?

```
```

2. In what kind of weather do you hear sounds like *crackle* and *crash*?

```
```

3. What kind of animal makes sounds like *chirp*, *tweet*, and *twitter*?

```
```

▶ **Pretend you are at a music concert. Make a list of all the sounds you hear.**

_____

_____

_____

© Harcourt

SYNONYMS

▶ Read each sentence. Find a word in the Word Box that is a synonym for the underlined word or words in the sentence. Write the word on the line. The first one is done for you.

famous	instrument	hear	concert	drums	flute

1. I love to <u>listen to</u> piano music. _____ hear _____

2. What kind of <u>tool</u> do you play? _____

3. Rosa plays a <u>woodwind</u>. _____

4. Carlos prefers to play <u>percussion instruments</u>. _____

5. Do you know any <u>well-known</u> musicians? _____

6. I enjoyed attending the <u>performance</u>. _____

▶ Now try these.

glad	practices	left	bother	tools	utensils

7. It's not polite to <u>disturb</u> people

   while they are listening to music. _____

8. James put <u>forks and spoons</u> on the table. _____

9. Ellen used the <u>devices</u> to fix her car. _____

10. We <u>departed</u> when the concert was over. _____

11. She was <u>pleased</u> when she got her new horn. _____

12. The musician <u>rehearses</u> every day. _____

Vocabulary Power

Name _____

COLORFUL WORDS

Colorful words make writing more interesting. Read each sentence part and its word choices. Write the most colorful word to complete each sentence part.

1. the _____ necklace

        pretty   sparkling

2. the _____ bunny

        fluffy   soft

3. the _____ star

        twinkling   bright

4. the _____ elephant

        big   enormous

5. the _____ candle

        glimmering   nice

6. the _____ snail

        slow   sluggish

7. the _____ water

        shimmering   pretty

8. the _____ jewel

        glistening   shiny

9. the _____ bear

        mean   fierce

10. the _____ ice-cream cone

        good   delicious

Name _____

WORD ENDINGS

Complete the word puzzles. Add the endings *-s, -ed,* and *-ing* to each word.

1. sparkle

   __ __ __ __ __ __ __ __

   __ __ __ __ __ __ __ __

   __ __ __ __ __ __ __ __ __

2. twinkle

   __ __ __ __ __ __ __ __

   __ __ __ __ __ __ __ __

3. glimmer

   __ __ __ __ __ __ __ __

   __ __ __ __ __ __ __ __

   __ __ __ __ __ __ __ __ __ __

4. glisten

   __ __ __ __ __ __ __ __

   __ __ __ __ __ __ __ __

   __ __ __ __ __ __ __ __ __

5. shimmer

   __ __ __ __ __ __ __ __

   __ __ __ __ __ __ __ __

   __ __ __ __ __ __ __ __ __ __

Vocabulary Power

Name _____

COMPARE AND CONTRAST

The words *glare* and *shimmer* are alike in some ways and different in others. Look at the diagram below. In the center circle, write the word from the Word Box that tells about both words. In the circle with *glare*, write the five words that tell only about *glare*. In the circle with *shimmer*, write the six words that tell only about *shimmer*.

harsh	gentle	soft	fierce
burn	glistening	sparkling	shine
bright	twinkling	uncomfortable	glimmering

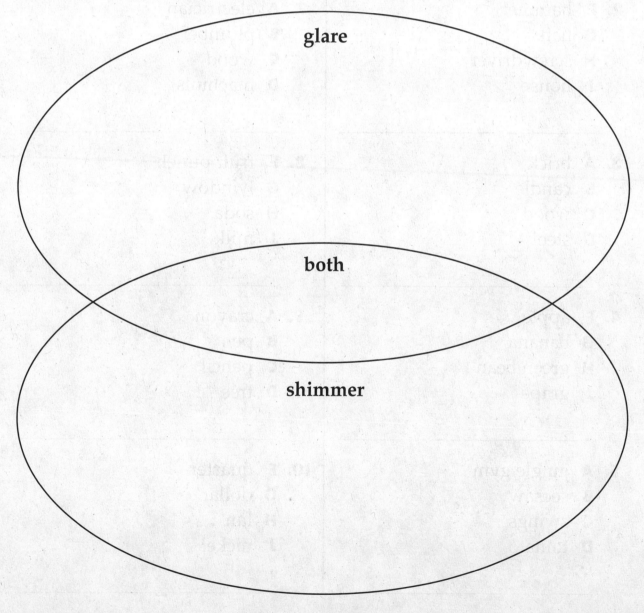

© Harcourt

Name _____

CLASSIFY/CATEGORIZE

Read each group of words below. Circle the letter of the word that does not belong in each group. Then add a category name for each group. The first one has been done for you.

1. A carpenter
 B mason
 (C) doctor
 D builder

 people who build things

2. F hammer
 G nails
 H screwdriver
 J house

 _____

3. A brick
 B candle
 C wood
 D steel

 _____

4. F apple
 G banana
 H green bean
 J grape

 _____

5. A jungle gym
 B seesaw
 C swings
 D tomato

 _____

6. F chair
 G toast
 H cereal
 J pancakes

 _____

7. A electrician
 B plumber
 C wood
 D machinist

 _____

8. F fruit punch
 G window
 H soda
 J milk

 _____

9. A crayon
 B pen
 C pencil
 D tree

 _____

10. F quarter
 G dollar
 H fan
 J nickel

 _____

Vocabulary Power

ANALOGIES

In an analogy, two pairs of words go together in the same way.

Examples:

The sun shines in the day. The moon shines at night.

Sun is to *day* as *moon* is to *night*.

▶ **Choose a word from the Word Box to complete each analogy.**

flowers	watch	wood	pipes	trees

1. A mason works with stone. A carpenter works with

   _____.

2. Apples are fruit. Roses are _____.

3. A beach has sand. A forest has _____.

4. An electrician fixes your electrical wiring. A plumber fixes your

   water _____.

5. A book is something you read. A television set is something

   you _____.

▶ **Now try these.**

wear	machines	sour	short	kitten

6. *Electricians* are to *electricity* as *machinists* are to _____.

7. *Hot* is to *cold* as *tall* is to _____.

8. *Food* is to *eat* as *clothes* are to _____.

9. *Sugar* is to *sweet* as *lemon* is to _____.

10. *Dog* is to *puppy* as *cat* is to _____.

Name _____

COMPARE AND CONTRAST

Complete the following statements

1. A *carpenter* is like a *mason* except _____

_____.

2. *Wood* is like *brick* because _____

_____.

3. A *plumber* is like an *electrician* except _____

_____.

4. A *hammer* is like a *wrench* because _____

_____.

5. A *fork* is like a *spoon* because _____

_____.

6. A *cabin* is like a *mansion* except _____

_____.

7. A *piano* is like a *flute* because _____

_____.

8. A *lake* is like an *ocean* except _____

_____.

9. A *quarter* is like a *dime* except _____

_____.

Vocabulary Power

EXPLORE WORD MEANING

Read and respond to each of the following questions or statements.

1. What books or stories have you read that are *fantasies*?

_____

_____

2. Would you rather read a story about *real* people or *imaginary* people?

_____

_____

3. What are some things that could happen in a *yarn* that couldn't happen in a true story?

_____

_____

4. What other characters might you read about in a *tale* about a

princess? _____

_____

5. Pretend you are writing a *fantasy* story. Draw a picture of the main character in your story. Then name your character.

_____

© Harcourt

DICTIONARY

Entry words in a dictionary are listed in alphabetical order. An entry word in a dictionary is followed by its pronunciation. Its part of speech is next. If there are two meanings, they are each numbered. Dictionaries sometimes include an example sentence to explain the meaning of the word.

Read the entries below. Then answer the questions.

> **imaginary** [i•maj′ə•ner•ē] *adj.* Existing only in the imagination, unreal.
>
> **pretend** [pri•tend′] *v.* To make believe: *Let's pretend we're movie stars.*
>
> **yarn** [yärn] *n.* **1.** Any spun strand. **2.** A made-up story.

1. How many syllables are in *imaginary*?

_____

2. Is a *yarn* a true story? How do you know?

_____

3. Why are there numerals in the meaning of *yarn*?

_____

4. Make up a new example sentence for *pretend*.

_____

5. Which word is pronounced this way? [i•maj′ə•ner•ē]

_____

6. Why is *yarn* the last word listed here?

_____

Vocabulary Power

© Harcourt

HOMOPHONES

▶ The words in each homophone pair below are pronounced the same but have different spellings and different meanings. Write the word from the Word Box that matches each clue below.

pear–pair	stare–stair	our–hour

Which word means . . .
1. "belongs to us"? _____

2. "sixty minutes"? _____

3. "a fruit"? _____

4. "two of something"? _____

5. "something you climb"? _____

6. "to look at"? _____

▶ Now try these.

tale–tail	mail–male	whole–hole

Which word means . . .
7. "what you dig"? _____

8. "all of something"? _____

9. "what a dog wags"? _____

10. "a story"? _____

11. "a letter"? _____

12. "a boy"? _____

Name _____

CONTEXT CLUES

Read each sentence, paying attention to the underlined word. Then answer the question about each word.

1. We got tickets for the big <u>event</u>.

What are three events you would need tickets for? _____

_____

2. I can't wait to <u>experience</u> the circus.
What are some words you could use in place of *experience*?

_____

_____

3. We had an <u>incident</u> in our class when our hamster got out.
What are some other incidents that happen during the school day?

_____

_____

4. Sue was in a fun <u>situation</u>. She got to meet a movie star!
What are some fun situations you have been in?

_____

_____

5. I can't wait to see the next <u>episode</u> of the show.
Tell about an episode of your favorite show.

_____

_____

Vocabulary Power

MULTIPLE-MEANING WORDS

▶ **Many words have more than one meaning. Clues from the sentence will tell you which meaning is being used. Read each sentence below. Circle the letter of the meaning of the underlined word.**

1. I had an interesting <u>experience</u> this morning.
   A something one has gone through
   B knowledge or skill gained by doing something

2. My uncle has two years of <u>experience</u> as a carpenter.
   A something one has gone through
   B knowledge or skill gained by doing something

3. He read the final <u>episode</u> of the play.
   A an event in history
   B one of a series of connected stories

4. I went to the <u>event</u> with my sister.
   A an important occasion
   B final outcome; result

5. When I get nervous, my hands <u>quiver</u>.
   A to make a trembling motion
   B a case for carrying arrows

6. Tammy made a <u>bolt</u> for the exit.
   A a rod for holding something in place
   B a sudden start

▶ **Write a sentence using one of the meanings of the word** *experience*. **Then have a partner read your sentence and write on a separate sheet of paper a definition for the meaning of** *experience* **you used.**

_____

_____

© Harcourt

SYNONYMS

▶ Read each word. Then write a word that means almost the same thing.

tale	incident	kids
exam	intelligent	shine

1. shimmer _____

2. test _____

3. smart _____

4. event _____

5. children _____

6. story _____

▶ Now try these.

creature	happy	motion picture
event	kind	angry

7. experience _____

8. glad _____

9. upset _____

10. animal _____

11. friendly _____

12. movie _____

PREFIXES

A prefix comes at the beginning of a word and changes the meaning of the word. For example, *pre-* in *precaution* makes the word mean "care taken before something happens." Below are some prefixes and their meanings.

pre-	before	*un-*	not
re-	again	*over-*	too much

Read each group of words below. Write the meaning for each word. The first one is done for you.

I. preheat: _____ heat before _____

2. overdo: _____

3. untold: _____

4. prepay: _____

5. uncut: _____

6. prejudge: _____

7. rewrap: _____

8. prehistoric: _____

9. overuse: _____

10. refilled: _____

11. unwashed: _____

12. overheat: _____

13. retell: _____

14. unsaid: _____

Name _____

WORD FAMILIES

▶ **Cross out the word in each group that does not belong. Then add another word to each group. The first one is done for you.**

I. prejudge	judgement	judged	~~prepare~~	judge
2. wash	warm	washed	prewash	_____
3. magnet	imagine	imagined	imagination	_____
4. precaution	cautious	careful	cautioning	_____
5. clear	clean	unclean	cleaning	_____
6. reuse	redo	used	useful	_____
7. spark	sparkly	sparkling	parking	_____
8. playful	playground	underground	player	_____

▶ **Now try these.**

9. fill	filled	film	refill	_____
10. historic	storage	prehistoric	historical	_____
11. test	pretest	retest	precut	_____
12. prepay	paying	paid	pain	_____
13. loading	reload	lead	overload	_____
14. heat	preheat	heal	heated	_____
15. hunter	hunger	hungry	hungrily	_____
16. taste	tasty	tasted	tassle	_____

Vocabulary Power

CONTEXT CLUES

Read each sentence. Then write a definition for each underlined word.

1. That fossil is so old that it's <u>prehistoric</u>.

_____

2. We will <u>prepay</u> for our tickets so we won't have to buy them when we get there.

_____

3. Sue <u>preheated</u> the oven before she baked the cookies.

_____

4. It isn't nice to <u>prejudge</u> people before you get to know them.

_____

5. We brought an umbrella as a <u>precaution</u> in case it rains.

_____

6. If you don't do it right, you will need to <u>redo</u> it.

_____

7. Studying is one way to <u>prepare</u> for a test.

_____

8. When my glass was empty, the waiter <u>refilled</u> it.

_____

Name _____

EXPLORE WORD MEANING

Read and answer each question. Use complete sentences.

1. Why is it important to get all of your nutrients?

_____

_____

2. Pretend you are a nutritionist. What are some things you would tell people to eat for breakfast?

_____

_____

3. Apples are an example of a carbohydrate. What are some other examples?

_____

_____

4. Chicken is an example of a protein. What are some other examples?

_____

_____

5. Is candy a nutritious food? Explain your answer.

_____

_____

6. What are some of your favorite nutritious foods?

_____

_____

　Vocabulary Power

Name _____

CONTENT-AREA WORDS

▶ **Read the information below. Then answer each question with the name of a nutrient.**

Nutrients help us stay healthy. There are six kinds of nutrients:
- **Proteins** are in meat, eggs, beans, and other foods.
- **Vitamins** help our bodies use other nutrients.
- **Minerals** are in milk, cheese, and other foods.
- **Fats** give us energy. However, too many fats are not good for us.
- **Carbohydrates** are in fruits, vegetables, and grains.
- **Water** helps nutrients move around our bodies and cools us off.

1. Which nutrient helps our body use other nutrients? _____

2. Which nutrient should we not eat a lot of? _____

3. Which nutrient cools us off on a hot day? _____

4. Which nutrient is found in fruits and vegetables? _____

5. Which nutrient is found in meat, eggs, and beans? _____

▶ **Draw a healthy meal. Make sure it includes all the nutrients.**

© Harcourt

CLASSIFY/CATEGORIZE

Put the words from the Word Box into the correct category. Then add two words of your own to each category.

peach	bread	eggs	beans
fish	potato	meat	cereal

carbohydrates	proteins
1. _____	_____
2. _____	_____
3. _____	_____
4. _____	_____
5. _____	_____
6. _____	_____

oranges	soda	chips	chicken
candy	peas	bread	gum

foods that are nutritious	foods that aren't nutritious
7. _____	_____
8. _____	_____
9. _____	_____
10. _____	_____
11. _____	_____
12. _____	_____

Vocabulary Power

Name _____

ANALOGIES

An analogy shows how pairs of words go together.

Examples:

A leaf is part of a tree; a petal is part of a flower.

Leaf is to *tree* as *petal* is to *flower*.

▶ **Read each analogy below. Then choose a word from the Word Box to complete the analogy.**

Tuesday	instrument	giggle	darken	clarify

1. *Excited* is the opposite of *bored*;

   lighten is the opposite of _____.

2. *Tired* is the same as *sleepy*;

   laugh is the same as _____.

3. *Cautious* is the same as *careful*;

   explain is the same as _____.

4. February and March are months;

   Monday and _____ are weekdays.

5. *Assistant* is the same as *helper*;

   tool is the same as _____.

▶ **Now try these.**

night	happy	plane

6. *Engineer* is to *train* as *pilot* is to _____.

7. *Glare* is to *angry* as *smile* is to _____.

8. *Forward* is to *backward* as *day* is to _____.

© Harcourt

Vocabulary Power

ANTONYMS AND SYNONYMS

▶ Read each word. Find its antonym in the Word Box and write it on the line. Then think of a synonym for the word and write it on the line.

quiet	slowly	wrap	confuse	darken

	Antonym	Synonym
1. brighten	_____	_____
2. clarify	_____	_____
3. noisy	_____	_____
4. swiftly	_____	_____
5. unwrap	_____	_____

▶ Now try these.

huge	frown	real	lose	sunny

	Antonym	Synonym
6. smile	_____	_____
7. find	_____	_____
8. rainy	_____	_____
9. imaginary	_____	_____
10. tiny	_____	_____

© Harcourt

Name _____

MULTIPLE-MEANING WORDS

▶ Many words have more than one meaning. Clues from the
sentence will help you figure out which meaning is being used.
Read each sentence below. Circle the letter of the meaning of the
underlined word.

1. Turn on the light to illuminate the room.
   A explain; clarify
   B light up

2. I had to take some clothes out to lighten my suitcase.
   A make bright
   B make less heavy

3. Grandpa told a yarn about his fishing trip.
   A made-up adventure story
   B thread used for knitting

4. We play in the park after school.
   A piece of land with trees and grass
   B to leave something standing somewhere for a time

5. Al looked at his watch to see what time it was.
   A to look at
   B something that shows the time

6. When my sister hears her favorite jingle, she sings along.
   A ringing sound
   B catchy song

▶ Write a sentence using the meaning of *illuminate* that you didn't
use above.

_____

_____

© Harcourt

Vocabulary Power

Name _____

SYNONYMS

▶ Look in the Word Box for pairs of words that are synonyms. Write a pair of synonyms on each line. The first one is done for you.

cavity	scowl	hollow	sprint	hill	run
slope	glossiest	crater	hole	frown	shiniest

1. _____ cavity/hole _____

2. _____

3. _____

4. _____

5. _____

6. _____

▶ Now try these.

glimmering	alike	shimmering	clarify	pile	gorge
connected	explain	similar	mound	chasm	fastened

7. _____

8. _____

9. _____

10. _____

11. _____

12. _____

Vocabulary Power

CLASSIFY/CATEGORIZE

▶ Read the headings below and the words in the Word Box. Write each word under the correct heading. Then add a word of your own to each category.

weakness	pain	energy
strength	smiles	fever

Signs of Good Health	Signs of Sickness
_____	_____
_____	_____
_____	_____

▶ Now try these.

hill	chasm	crater
gorge	mound	bump

Kinds of Holes	Kinds of Raised Land
_____	_____
_____	_____
_____	_____

Name _____

MULTIPLE-MEANING WORDS

Some words have more than one meaning. Clues from the sentence
tell you which meaning is being used. Read each pair of sentences
below. Write the letter of the correct meaning next to each sentence.

1. _____ The dentist said I have a <u>cavity</u>.

_____ Does a squirrel live in that <u>cavity</u>?

A a hollow space
B decay in a tooth

2. _____ A hungry bear will <u>gorge</u> itself.

_____ Looking down into
the <u>gorge</u> was scary.

A to stuff with food
B a very deep, narrow
valley

3. _____ The book weighs about
a <u>pound</u>.

_____ I will <u>pound</u> the nail.

A measure of heaviness
B hit

4. _____ This chocolate is <u>hollow</u>.

_____ The rabbit lives in the <u>hollow</u>.

A a hole
B empty inside

5. _____ I'm a big <u>fan</u> of that singer.

_____ The <u>fan</u> cooled us.

A machine that blows air
B an admirer

6. _____ The bully is really <u>mean</u>!

_____ What does *aboard* <u>mean</u>?

A a definition
B nasty, not nice

7. _____ There was a traffic <u>jam</u> today.

_____ I like <u>jam</u> on my toast.

A something blocking
movement
B a fruit spread

8. _____ You can't <u>fool</u> me.

_____ Sometimes I act like a <u>fool</u>.

A trick
B silly person

Vocabulary Power

Name _____

WORD FAMILIES

▶ Word families are made up of words that have the same root or base word. Read the words below. Circle the letter of the word that does not belong.

1. **A** vaccine
   B vacation
   C vaccination
   D vaccinate

2. **F** treatment
   G treat
   H treaty
   J treasure

3. **A** medicine
   B medical
   C media
   D medicate

4. **F** light
   G flight
   H lighten
   J lightning

5. **A** money
   B harmony
   C harmonious
   D harmonica

6. **F** part
   G partly
   H partner
   J artistic

▶ Use a word from the Word Box to complete each sentence.

injection	remedy

7. Is chicken soup a _____ for a cold?

8. Did you get the vaccine as an _____?

▶ Now write your own sentence using the word *vaccine*.

9. _____

_____

Name _____

CLASSIFY/CATEGORIZE

Read each group of words. Each group has special words that are all about one topic. Circle the letter next to the correct topic. Then add a word to each group of words.

I. vaccines, healthy food, washing hands, _____
- **A** things that make us sick
- **B** things to do on weekends
- **C** birthday gifts
- **D** things that keep us healthy

2. crayons, paper, glue, _____
- **F** things for a pet
- **G** art and craft supplies
- **H** homework
- **J** things with which to clean the house

3. tag, kickball, catch, _____
- **A** games to play outside
- **B** favorite books
- **C** games to play inside
- **D** favorite videos

4. sneezing, sore throat, fever, _____
- **F** signs of health
- **G** things to get vaccinated against
- **H** signs of sickness
- **J** things on a shopping list

5. remedy, treatment, injection, _____
- **A** favorite foods
- **B** games to play outside
- **C** sports teams
- **D** things that help us when we're sick

Vocabulary Power

© Harcourt

IDIOMS

An idiom is a group of words. The meaning of the group of words is usually different from the meaning of each word. Read and illustrate each idiom. Then use the idioms to complete the sentences below.

▶

1. a shot in the arm	**2.** catch your breath
3. got cold feet	**4.** get a taste of your own medicine

▶ **5.** The good news was _____.

6. Before the dive, she _____.

7. Stop running and _____.

8. If you aren't nice to others, you might _____

_____.

CONTEXT CLUES

Read each sentence, paying attention to the underlined word. Then answer the question about that word.

1. John's mom asked him to <u>assist</u> her with the dishes.
What are some things you assist your family with?

_____

_____

2. The coach told us <u>teamwork</u> would help us win the game.
What are some sports or games where teamwork is used?

_____

_____

3. The teacher gave each student a <u>partner</u> to do the project with.
How can having a partner be helpful?

_____

4. Emily is going to <u>cooperate</u> with Anne to write a story.
What does *cooperate* mean?

_____

_____

5. Our teacher said our class will <u>collaborate</u> with the other third-grade class to put on a play.
What are some other projects you could collaborate on?

_____

_____

Vocabulary Power

ANALOGIES

An analogy shows how pairs of words go together.

Example:

A broom is used for sweeping; a cloth is used for dusting.
Broom is to *sweeping* as *cloth* is to *dusting*.

▶ **Read each analogy below. Then choose a word from the Word Box to complete the analogy, and write it on the line.**

help	cutting	number	flies	low

1. *Cooperate* is the opposite of *fight*;

   high is the opposite of _____.

2. An *instrument* is the same as a *device*;

   assist is the same as _____.

3. *Blue* is a *color*; *two* is a _____.

4. *Pencils* are used for *writing*; *scissors* are used for _____.

5. A *shark swims*; an *eagle* _____.

▶ **Now try these.**

flower	rock	drink	partner	talk

6. *Running* is to *jogging* as *companion* is to _____.

7. *Basketball* is to *game* as *daisy* is to _____.

8. *Sandwich* is to *eat* as *water* is to _____.

9. *Beach* is to *sand* as *mountain* is to _____.

10. *Working together* is to *collaborate* as *speak* is to _____.

COMPOUND WORDS

A compound word is two words put together to form a new word. Read the compound word in Column A. Then use the beginning word in each compound word to form a new word in Column B.

Example:

Column A	Column B
teamwork	teammate

	Column A	Column B
1.	sunrise	sun_____
2.	bookcase	book_____
3.	outdoors	out_____
4.	everyone	every_____
5.	footstep	foot_____
6.	notepad	note_____
7.	campfire	camp_____
8.	overdone	over_____
9.	fireplace	fire_____
10.	doorstep	door_____
11.	upstairs	up_____
12.	anyone	any_____
13.	heartbeat	heart_____
14.	headline	head_____

Vocabulary Power

© Harcourt

SYNONYMS

▶ Look in the Word Box for pairs of words that are synonyms. Write a pair of synonyms on each line. The first one is done for you.

beliefs	special	pasture	jump	procedures	customs
traditions	ideas	ceremonies	unusual	leap	meadow

1. _____ traditions/customs _____

2. _____

3. _____

4. _____

5. _____

6. _____

▶ Now try these.

nervous	sparkle	practices	twinkle	trade	plain
assist	habits	ordinary	worried	exchange	help

7. _____

8. _____

9. _____

10. _____

11. _____

12. _____

CONTEXT CLUES

▶ **Read each sentence. Then write a definition for the underlined word.**

   I. One of my <u>practices</u> is to have a good breakfast every morning.

_____

_____

   2. Blowing out candles on birthday cakes is a common <u>custom</u>.

_____

_____

   3. One of Joe's <u>beliefs</u> is that it's good to be kind to others.

_____

_____

   4. People get married at wedding <u>ceremonies</u>.

_____

_____

   5. Playing games on Friday night is a <u>tradition</u> in Ellen's family.

_____

_____

▶ **What is a tradition you would like to start in your family?**

_____

_____

© Harcourt

WORD ORIGINS

Tradition comes from a Latin word that means "handing over." Families "hand over" their traditions to their children.

Look at the word web below. Fill in as many examples as you can for each kind of tradition. You could list your family's traditions or ones you have heard about, read about, or seen on television.

Places That People Go Every Year
Example: zoo

_____

_____

_____

Holidays That People Celebrate
Example: Kwanzaa

_____

_____

_____

Ceremonies That People Attend
Example: graduations

_____

_____

Traditions

Games That People Play
Example: dreidel

_____

_____

Food That People Eat at Special Times
Example: cake on birthdays

_____

_____

_____

© Harcourt

Name _____

PREFIXES

Use the prefixes from the list below to make new words. The first one is done for you.

dis- not or absence of		mis- wrong or wrongly	
re- again		un- not	

Beginning Word	Directions	New Word
1. registered	Add a prefix to mean "registered again."	reregistered
2. open	Add a prefix to mean "not opened."	_____
3. apply	Add a prefix to mean "apply again."	_____
4. easy	Add a prefix to mean "not easy."	_____
5. enlist	Add a prefix to mean "enlist again."	_____
6. understand	Add a prefix to mean "wrongly understand."	_____
7. enroll	Add a prefix to mean "enroll again."	_____
8. encourage	Change the prefix to mean "not having courage."	_____
9. requested	Add a prefix to mean "not requested."	_____

Vocabulary Power

RHYMING WORDS

▶ Use words from the Word Box to complete the sentences below. The word you write should rhyme with the underlined word in the sentence.

whale	noon	treat	test	bright	mason	enroll

1. Stand by the <u>pole</u> if you want to _____ for soccer.

2. The <u>cartoon</u> comes on at _____.

3. <u>Preheat</u> the oven before you make the _____.

4. John will <u>request</u> to take the _____.

5. The <u>light</u> was very _____.

6. Did you hear the <u>tale</u> about the _____?

7. <u>Jason</u> plans to be a _____.

▶ Now try these.

enlist	show	pain	twirled	apply	event	shimmering

8. Jennie will <u>cry</u> if you don't _____ to be in her club.

9. Do you <u>know</u> when the _____ starts?

10. The doctor will <u>explain</u> the _____ in my foot.

11. I <u>insist</u> that you _____ for the project.

12. Were you <u>sent</u> to the _____?

13. The stars were <u>glimmering</u> and _____ in the evening sky.

14. The ballerina <u>swirled</u> and _____ across the stage.

© Harcourt

WORD ENDINGS

Words can have several endings, depending on how they are used in a sentence. Read each sentence below. Then circle the letter of the word with the correct ending.

1. Have you _____ for summer camp yet?
    A register
    B registering
    C registered
    D registers

2. I will _____ tomorrow.
    F enroll
    G enrolls
    H enrolling
    J enrolled

3. I am _____ a cookie for dessert.
    A request
    B requested
    C requests
    D requesting

4. My sister is _____ for a job.
    F apply
    G applying
    H applies
    J applied

5. My uncles _____ in many activities.
    A enlist
    B enlisting
    C enlists
    D enlisted

RELATED WORDS

You have just opened your own pizza place. Follow the directions to create advertisements for your new restaurant.

1. Draw a logo to put on T-shirts. Include the name of your restaurant.

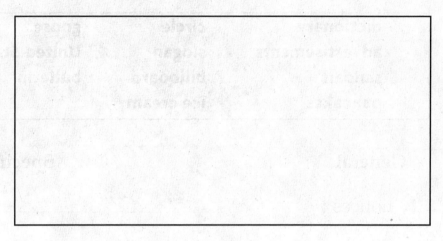

2. Write a slogan to put on the cover of your menu.

_____

3. Create a billboard for your restaurant.

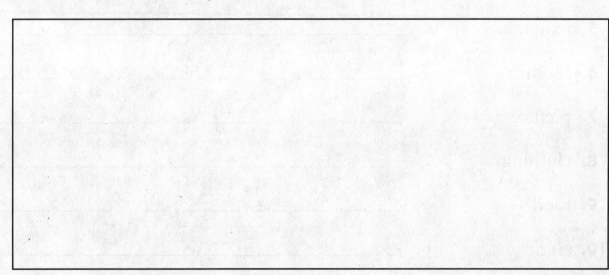

4. Write an ad for your restaurant that could be included in your community's monthly bulletin. Include rhyming words.

_____

_____

Name _____

GENERAL AND SPECIFIC NOUNS

Read each word. Choose a more specific noun from the Word Box
and write it on the line.

dictionary	circle	goose	shirt
advertisements	slogan	United States	kitchen
sandals	billboard	bulletin	logo
pancakes	ice cream		

General   **Specific**

1. notices   _____

2. bird   _____

3. saying   _____

4. book   _____

5. magazine   _____

6. room   _____

7. picture   _____

8. clothing   _____

9. food   _____

10. sign   _____

11. shape   _____

12. country   _____

13. dessert   _____

14. shoes   _____

Vocabulary Power

Name _____

SUFFIXES

Suffixes can be added to the ends of words to change their meanings. Below are some suffixes and their meanings.

-less	without	-ful	full of
-ment	result of condition	-en	make to be
-ness	state or condition	-er, -or	one who

Read each sentence below. Choose the word in parentheses ( ) with the correct suffix. Write it on the line. The first one is done for you.

1. Julie wanted to sell her old bike, so she wrote an

_____advertisement_____. **(advertiser, advertisement)**

2. A billboard can be _____ when you're advertising. **(helpful, helpless)**

3. Do not be _____ when you use scissors. **(careful, careless)**

4. Each board must be the correct _____. **(thicken, thickness)**

5. He works for the national _____. **(governor, government)**

6. Add color to the logo to _____ it up. **(brighten, brightness)**

7. Kelly considered the question for a long time. She was

_____. **(thoughtless, thoughtful)**

8. This game needs another _____. **(playful, player)**

9. Adding white paint to the red paint will make it

_____. **(lighten, lighter)**

© Harcourt

Name _____

COMPARE AND CONTRAST

The words *monarchy* and *republic* are alike in some ways and different in others. Look at the diagram below. In the center circle, write the word from the Word Box that tells about both words. In the circle with *monarchy*, write the five words that tell only about *monarchy*. In the circle with *republic*, write the five words that tell only about *republic*.

royalty	king	election
President	government	democracy
voting	queen	throne
kingdom	federal	

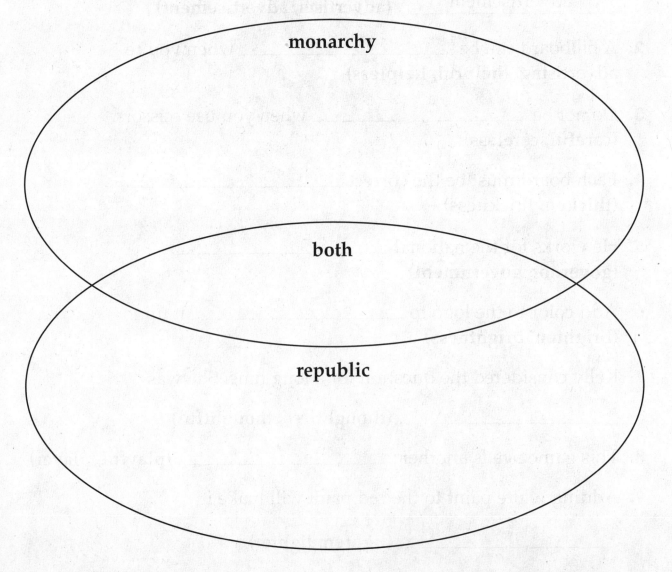

Vocabulary Power

© Harcourt

CLASSIFY/CATEGORIZE

▶ Cross out the word in each group that does not belong. Then add another word to each group. The groups are based on the meanings of the words.

1. state   federal   New York   local   _____

2. senator   mayor   governor   teacher   _____

3. choose   vote   sing   decide   _____

4. president   monarchy   king   queen   _____

5. republic   prince   election   voting   _____

6. California   Nebraska   Alaska   Canada   _____

7. China   Utah   Italy   France   _____

▶ Now try these. The groups are based on the word endings.

8. listened   respond   studied   decided   _____

9. finishing   voting   serving   talked   _____

10. discussing   repairing   helped   providing   _____

11. visited   will invite   changed   increased   _____

12. talked   continued   selected   listen   _____

13. swimmer   dancer   running   jumper   _____

14. cleans   runs   elects   moved   _____

Name _____

EXPLORE WORD MEANING

Read and answer each question. Use complete sentences.

1. A mayor is a leader in a local government. What are some leaders in the federal government? _____

_____

2. Which kind of government would you rather have—a monarchy or a democracy? Explain your answer. _____

_____

3. What are some jobs the President might have to do?

_____

_____

4. Why do you think we have a government?

_____

_____

5. If you were the President, what are some things you would do?

_____

_____

6. Why do you think it is important to vote?

_____

_____

Vocabulary Power

CONTEXT CLUES

▶ **Circle the words in each sentence that help give the meaning of the underlined word. On the line, write the word's meaning.**

1. The people in our <u>community</u> all live near one another.

Community means _____.

2. The <u>population</u> of our house is five people.

Population means _____.

3. The small <u>settlement</u> has houses and a grocery store.

Settlement means _____.

4. Our town is divided into six <u>neighborhoods</u>.

Neighborhood means _____.

5. Bees are <u>social</u> insects because they live in large groups.

Social means _____.

REGIONALISMS

▶ **Read each sentence and the words in parentheses. Underline the word you would use in the sentence. All of the words are used by people in different communities, so all of the words are correct.**

6. At home, we sit on a **(sofa, couch)**.

7. For breakfast, some people eat **(batter cakes, pancakes, flapjacks)**.

8. You can carry groceries in a **(bag, sack, poke)**.

9. You can carry water in a **(bucket, pail)**.

Name _____

WORD FAMILIES

Word families are made up of words that have the same root or base word. Read each set of words below. Circle the letter of the word that does not belong. Then replace it with another word.

1. **A** neighbor
   B neighborhood
   C unneighborly
   D unfriendly

   _____

2. **F** community
   G confuse
   H communicate
   J communicable

   _____

3. **A** populate
   B popular
   C popcorn
   D population

4. **F** cavern
   G govern
   H government
   J governing

5. **A** explain
   B explanation
   C explained
   D excited

   _____

6. **F** select
   G settlement
   H settler
   J settled

   _____

7. **A** social
   B sociable
   C socially
   D socket

8. **F** prairie
   G practices
   H practical
   J practiced

Vocabulary Power

Name_____

EXPLORE WORD MEANING

Every community is a little bit different. Look at the word web below. Describe your community by filling in as many examples as you can for each category. When you are finished, you may want to compare your answers with those of your classmates.

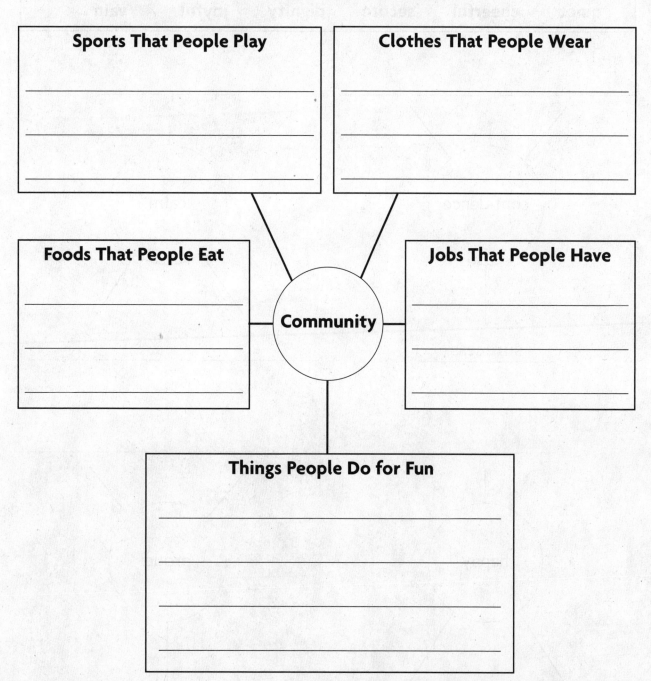

Sports That People Play

_____

_____

_____

Clothes That People Wear

_____

_____

_____

Foods That People Eat

_____

_____

_____

Community

Jobs That People Have

_____

_____

_____

Things People Do for Fun

_____

_____

_____

_____

Name_____

SYNONYMS

You can make word webs of synonyms. Write each word from the
Word Box around its synonym. One word is written for you.

still	sureness	glad	relaxed	haughty	certainty
quiet	cheerful	secure	dignity	joyful	vain

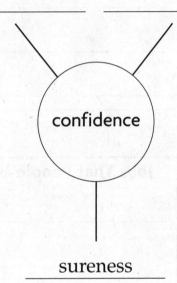

confidence

sureness

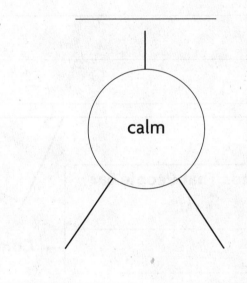

calm

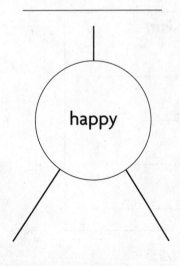

happy

proud

Vocabulary Power

© Harcourt

Name _____

HOMOPHONES

Choose the letter of the correct meaning for each word and write it on the line. Then write a sentence using the two words.

1. ate: _____   eight: _____
   A had a meal
   B a number

_____

2. vain: _____   vein: _____
   A too proud
   B vessel that carries blood

_____

3. week: _____   weak: _____
   A not strong
   B seven days

_____

4. hair: _____   hare: _____
   A a rabbit
   B grows on your head

_____

5. blue: _____   blew: _____
   A a color
   B what the wind did

_____

Name _____

COMPARE AND CONTRAST

▶ Look at the diagram below. In the center circle, write the word
from the Word Box that tells about both words. In the circle with
haughtiness, write the three words that tell only about *haughtiness*.
In the circle with *confidence*, write the three words that tell only
about *confidence*.

vain	pride	dignity	trust
arrogant	secure	scornful	

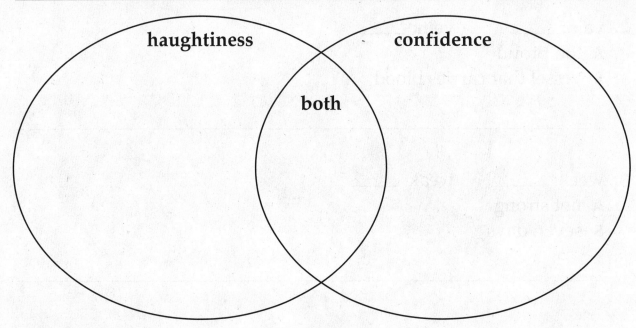

haughtiness   confidence

both

▶ Answer each question. You may wish to use some of the words
from above to help you.

1. What are some words to describe someone who is always looking

in the mirror? _____

_____

2. What are some things a person with confidence might do?

_____

_____

Vocabulary Power

ANALOGIES

▶ **Read each analogy below. Then choose a word from the Word Box to complete the analogy, and write it on the line.**

ground	science	stars	night	earth

1. Biology is the study of life; astronomy is the study of

   _____.

2. The earth goes around the sun; the moon goes around the

   _____.

3. A star is in the sky; soil is on the _____.

4. Addition is part of math; astronomy is part of

   _____.

5. The sun can be seen during the day; stars can be seen at

   _____.

▶ **Now try these.**

hot	galaxy	disharmony	meteor	water

6. *Planets* are to *solar system* as *solar system* is to

   _____.

7. *Forests* are to *trees* as *oceans* are to _____.

8. *Piece* is to *whole* as *meteorite* is to _____.

9. *Ice* is to *cold* as *sun* is to _____.

10. *Agreement* is to *disagreement* as *harmony* is to

    _____.

CLASSIFY/CATEGORIZE

▶ Read the categories below. Write each word from the Word Box in the correct category. Then add five words of your own to each category.

soil	galaxies	meteors	stars	planets
trees	solar system	earthworms	rocks	roots

Things in Space	Things In or On the Ground
I. _____	_____
2. _____	_____
3. _____	_____
4. _____	_____
5. _____	_____
6. _____	_____
7. _____	_____
8. _____	_____
9. _____	_____
10. _____	_____

▶ On your own sheet of paper, draw a picture to illustrate one word from each category.

© Harcourt

Name _____

SEQUENCE

Read each group of words and place them on the scale in the correct order.

1. From smallest to largest: solar system, universe, galaxy, planet

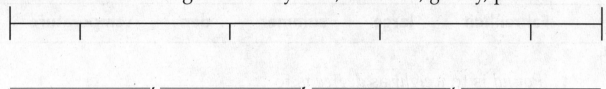

_____ , _____ , _____ , _____

2. From smallest to largest: city, continent, state, country

_____ , _____ , _____ , _____

3. From earliest to latest: noon, morning, night, sunset

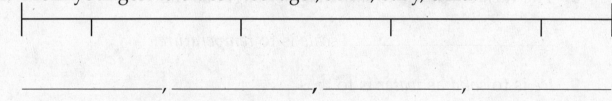

_____ , _____ , _____ , _____

4. From youngest to oldest: teenager, adult, baby, child

_____ , _____ , _____ , _____

© Harcourt

ANALOGIES

▶ **Read each analogy below. Think about how the first two italicized words go together. Then write the word from the Word Box that completes the analogy.**

Fahrenheit	large	summer	den	temperature

I. *Pound* is to *weight* as *degree* is to _____.

2. *Short* is to *tall* as *small* is to _____.

3. *Winter* is to *cold* as _____ is to *hot*.

4. *Volt* is to *electricity* as _____ *scale* is to *temperature*.

5. *Bird* is to *nest* as *lion* is to _____.

▶ **Now try these.**

day	liquid	tasting	mercury	Celsius

6. *Light* is to *dark* as *night* is to _____.

7. *Pages* are to *book* as _____ is to *thermometer*.

8. The *Richter scale* is to *earthquake strength* as the

_____ *scale* is to *temperature*.

9. *Ice* is to *solid* as *water* is to _____.

10. *Ears* are to *hearing* as *tongue* is to _____.

Vocabulary Power

ABBREVIATIONS

▶ Complete the chart by writing the word from the Word Box that goes with each abbreviation.

Fahrenheit	Doctor	millimeter	centimeter	Avenue	ounce

ABBREVIATION	WORD
1. oz.	
2. Ave.	
3. F	
4. Dr.	
5. cm	
6. mm	

▶ Complete the chart by writing the abbreviation from the Word Box that goes with each word.

Wed.	C	Mr.	mi.	Oct.	km

ABBREVIATION	WORD
7.	Celsius
8.	Wednesday
9.	Mister
10.	October
11.	mile
12.	kilometer

GENERAL AND SPECIFIC NOUNS

Read each word. Choose a more specific noun from the Word Box and write it on the line. Then add your own word.

Celsius scale	degree	summer	Earth	wedding
democracy	animated film	mercury	astronomy	mountain
hollow	yarn	jingle	President	

General	Specific	
1. story	_____	_____
2. hole	_____	_____
3. temperature scale	_____	_____
4. unit of measure	_____	_____
5. landform	_____	_____
6. government	_____	_____
7. leader	_____	_____
8. science	_____	_____
9. planet	_____	_____
10. movie	_____	_____
11. ceremony	_____	_____
12. element	_____	_____
13. season	_____	_____
14. song	_____	_____

Vocabulary Power

Name _____

SYNONYMS

Synonyms are words that have similar meanings. Read each group of words below. Circle the letter of the word that is a synonym of the underlined word.

1. blustery
   A bluff
   B gusty
   C weather
   D mystery

2. false
   F calls
   G fame
   H true
   J untrue

3. breezy
   A cloudy
   B sunny
   C windy
   D rainy

4. excuse
   F reason
   G expect
   H examine
   J misuse

5. tremble
   A trickle
   B tumble
   C shake
   D example

6. doldrums
   F blustery
   G thunder
   H blizzard
   J stillness

7. tranquil
   A excited
   B calm
   C train
   D noisy

8. limbs
   F branches
   G trees
   H evergreens
   J limp

9. splinter
   A sprinkle
   B split
   C splash
   D splendid

10. scatter
   F schedule
   G scare
   H spread
   J scarf

© Harcourt

Name _____

EXPLORE WORD MEANING

▶ **Read and respond to each question.**

1. A blustery day is loud and windy. How might a blustery person

act? _____

_____

2. *Tranquil* means "calm and peaceful." What are some things that

are tranquil? _____

_____

3. How does someone who is "in the doldrums" feel?

_____

_____

4. A sunny day is bright and warm. How do you feel when you're

in a sunny mood? _____

_____

▶ **Illustrate the following kinds of people.**

a blustery person	a tranquil person

Name _____

SUFFIXES

Below are some suffixes and their meanings.

Suffix	Meaning	Suffix	Meaning
-less	without	-y	like
-ness	state or condition	-ly	like
-ful	filled with	-en	make to be

Read each sentence. Choose the correct suffix to add to the underlined word in parentheses. The words in parentheses are clues to help you decide which suffix should be used. Write the new word on the line. The first one is done for you.

1. He is a kind and _____thoughtful_____ person. **(filled with thought)**

2. Today, the wind is _____. **(gust-like)**

3. Yesterday, it was _____. **(breeze-like)**

4. Some sunshine would _____ this day. **(make to be bright)**

5. Outside, it was cold and _____. **(bluster-like)**

6. Would you _____ pass the salt? **(kind-like)**

7. Her heart is full of _____. **(condition of being kind)**

8. I was _____ to forget your birthday. **(without thought)**

9. The sky began to _____. **(make to be dark)**

10. There was _____ all around us. **(state of being dark)**

© Harcourt

CLASSIFY/CATEGORIZE

▶ Write each word from the Word Box under the correct category.
Then write your own word for each category.

computers	relationships	habitat
snakes	environment	alligators
reptiles	software	microchips

     herpetology   ecology   technology

_____   _____   _____

_____   _____   _____

_____   _____   _____

▶ Now try these.

ancient cities	mammals	flowers
trees	culture	ruins

        biology   archaeology

     _____   _____

     _____   _____

     _____   _____

Name _____

DICTIONARY

Use the dictionary entry below to answer the following questions.

e•col•o•gy [ē•kol′ə•jē] *n.* **1.** The study of how living things relate to their surroundings. **2.** The balance between living things and their sur-roundings. —ecologist, *n.*

1. Which of these shows the correct syllable to stress in *ecology*? Circle the letter of the correct answer.

    A ē•kol•ə′•jē
    B ē′kol•ə•jē
    C ē•kol′ə•jē
    D ē•kol•ə•jē′

2. How many meanings does *ecology* have? _____

3. What part of speech is *ecology*? _____

4. What word is based on *ecology* in the dictionary entry? _____

5. If the suffix *-ist* means "a person," what do you think *ecologist* means?

_____

_____

6. Write a sentence using *ecology*.

_____

_____

7. Write a sentence using *ecologist*.

_____

_____

WORD PARTS

Add the root and the suffix together to create a word. Then use the meaning of each word part to write a definition for the word.

Suffixes		Roots	
-logy	the study of	*archaeo*	ancient
-ist	a person who makes or studies	*bio*	living things
		chrono	time
		eco	environment
		herpeto	reptiles
		psycho	mind

1. eco + logy = _____

_____

2. bio + logy = _____

_____

3. archaeo + logy = _____

_____

4. herpeto + logy = _____

_____

5. chrono + logy – y + ist = _____

_____

6. psycho + logy – y + ist = _____

_____

What are some other *-logy* or *-ist* words?

_____

Vocabulary Power

CONTEXT CLUES

▶ **Read each sentence, paying attention to the underlined word. Then complete the statements about the underlined words.**

1. Susan's <u>canine</u> barks and wags its tail.

A canine is a _____.

2. John's <u>feline</u> meows when it is hungry.

A feline is a _____.

3. The <u>porcine</u> animal oinks and eats a lot.

Porcine means _____.

4. The <u>bovine</u> moos and produces milk.

A bovine is a _____.

5. The <u>equine</u> has a brown mane and a flowing tail.

An equine is a _____.

▶ **Use each letter of the animal's name to write a word that describes it. The word can describe the way the animal looks, acts, or sounds. One example for each animal is done for you.**

F _____ furry _____   C _____

E _____   A _____

L _____   N _____

I _____   I _____

N _____   N _____

E _____   E _____ energetic _____

© Harcourt

RELATED WORDS

Many groups of animals have "family names." Dogs are part of the canine family. Cats, including pets and wild cats, are felines. Cows are bovines. Horses are in the equine family.

Write the correct family name for each animal above its picture. Then write each word from the Word Box under the correct picture. Finally, add your own example for each animal.

dog	lion	steer	colt	cow
wolf	horse	zebra	cattle	coyote
cat	kitten			

Vocabulary Power

© Harcourt

Name _____

ANALOGIES

An analogy shows how pairs of words go together.

Example:
Hot is to *cold* as *day* is to *night.*
(*Hot* is the opposite of *cold*; *day* is the opposite of *night*.)

▶ **Read each analogy below. Figure out how the first two italicized words go together. Then write the word that completes the analogy.**

1. *Porcine* is to *pig* as *canine* is to _____.

2. *Bovine* is to *cow* as *equine* is to _____.

3. *Canine* is to *bark* as *feline* is to _____.

4. *Oink* is to *porcine* as *neigh* is to _____.

5. *Wolf* is to *canine* as *tiger* is to _____.

6. *Calf* is to *cow* as *kitten* is to _____.

7. *Fish* are to *gills* as *people* are to _____.

▶ **Now try these.**

8. *Pig* is to *corn* as *horse* is to _____.

9. *Dog* is to *house* as *pig* is to _____.

10. *Four legs* are to *cats* as *two legs* are to _____.

11. *Fur* is to *animals* as _____ are to *birds.*

12. *Paws* are to *canines* as _____ are to *equines.*

13. *Snouts* are to *pigs* as _____ are to *people.*

14. *Camel* is to *desert* as *stingray* is to _____.

Name _____

COMPARE AND CONTRAST

Complete the following statements.

1. An *evergreen* is like a *deciduous tree* except _____

_____.

2. An *annual* is like a *biennial* except _____

_____.

3. A *perennial* is like an *annual* because _____

_____.

4. A *farmer* is like a *gardener* because _____

_____.

5. An *orange* is like a *lemon* except _____

_____.

6. A *year* is like a *month* except _____

_____.

7. *Flowers* are like *trees* because _____

_____.

8. A *horse* is like a *pony* except _____

_____.

9. *Walking* is like *running* because _____

_____.

Vocabulary Power

Name _____

COMPOUND WORDS

Read the compound word in Column A. Then use the beginning word in each compound word to form a new word in Column B.

Example:

Column A   **Column B**

evergreen   everlasting

1. outside   out_____

2. downtown   down_____

3. anyway   any_____

4. housework   house_____

5. homemade   home_____

6. everything   every_____

7. overhead   over_____

8. farmhouse   farm_____

9. underground   under_____

10. earthworm   earth_____

11. ice cream   ice_____

12. upstream   up_____

13. waterproof   water_____

14. landslide   land_____

© Harcourt

Vocabulary Power

CONTEXT CLUES

▶ **Read each sentence. Then write a definition for the underlined word.**

1. I have had my <u>perennial</u> plant for many years.

_____

2. The <u>deciduous</u> tree lost its leaves when winter came.

_____

3. The <u>annual</u> plant only lived for one year.

_____

4. The leaves of the <u>evergreen</u> are always green.

_____

5. The <u>biennial</u> plant lived for two years.

_____

6. I thought the <u>everlasting</u> movie would never end.

_____

▶ **Pick two of the underlined words from above. Write one sentence for each word.**

7. _____

_____

8. _____

_____

Vocabulary Power

CLASSIFY/CATEGORIZE

Read each group of words below. Circle the letter of the word or phrase that does not belong in each group. Then name each category.

1. A crops
B rural
C agricultural
D city

_____

2. F kitchen
G bedroom
H outside
J living room

_____

3. A apartments
B undeveloped
C skyscrapers
D offices

_____

4. F green
G blue
H soft
J purple

_____

5. A museum
B rustic
C natural
D meadow

_____

6. F lake
G river
H desert
J ocean

_____

7. A hot
B pink
C warm
D cold

_____

8. F computer
G campsite
H tent
J hiking

_____

9. A mother
B brother
C sister
D friend

_____

10. F dog
G tiger
H cat
J goldfish

_____

© Harcourt

Name _____

COMPARE AND CONTRAST

The words *country* and *city* are alike in some ways and different in others. Look at the diagram below. In the center circle, write the word from the Word Box that tells about both words. In the circle with *country*, write the five words that have to do with *country*. In the circle with *city*, write the five words that have to do with *city*.

places	rustic	rural	agricultural
traffic	natural	skyscrapers	undeveloped
busy	developed	noisy	

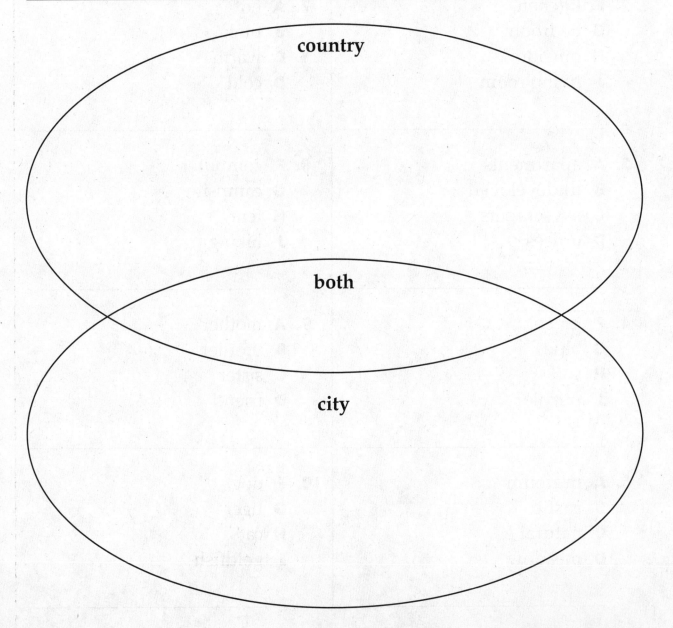

off© Harcourt

SYNONYMS AND ANTONYMS

▶ Read the words below. For each word, choose a synonym and an antonym from the Word Box. Write these words on the lines. The first one is done for you.

scared	country	warm	right	large
small	wrong	city	cold	brave

	Synonym	Antonym
1. rural	country	city
2. big		
3. hot		
4. afraid		
5. correct		

▶ Now try these.

undeveloped	lose	beat	healthy	new
built up	rude	thoughtful	aged	sick

	Synonym	Antonym
6. polite		
7. developed		
8. win		
9. old		
10. ill		

Name _____

RELATED WORDS

Every type of career has jobs that are related to it. Underneath each category, draw a picture that represents it. Then write each job from the Word Box underneath the type of career it is related to. Finally, add a job to each list.

paramedic	paralegal	referee	coach	doctor
singer	trainer	lawyer	legal secretary	actress
comedian	nurse	actor	surgeon	basketball player

Athletic Careers	Medical Careers	Legal Careers	Entertainment Careers

Vocabulary Power

Name _____

EXPLORE WORD MEANING

▶ **Read and respond to each question. Use complete sentences.**

1. What are some special skills that people with careers in athletics

   need to have? _____

   _____

2. What kind of personality do you think you would need if you

   wanted a legal career? _____

   _____

3. When might you need to see someone who has a medical career?

   _____

   _____

4. There are many different entertainment careers. In what type of
   entertainment career would you be most interested? Why?

   _____

   _____

▶ **Rank the types of careers from one to four. Your number-one
   career should be the one in which you are most interested. Your
   number-four career should be the one in which you are least
   interested. Then explain the reason for your order.**

   _____ athletic   _____ legal

   _____ entertainment   _____ medical

   _____

   _____

WORD FAMILIES

▶ The word *career* is based on a word that means "car." All the words below are in the same family because they come from this word. Read the words and their meanings. Then use each word to complete one of the sentences. You will use one word twice.

car	a vehicle that takes you places
career	work that takes you through life
carriage	a fancy kind of wagon pulled by a horse
carry	to move something from one place to another
chariots	carts with two wheels, pulled by horses; used long ago in races

1. My uncle has a _____ in agriculture.

2. We drove to Florida in our _____.

3. The ancient Romans raced each other in their _____.

4. A horse pulled our _____ in a ride around the park.

5. You are too heavy for me to _____.

6. My sister has a _____ in medicine.

▶ Use two of the words in the list above in sentences of your own.

7. _____

    _____

8. _____

    _____

Vocabulary Power

Name _____

MULTIPLE-MEANING WORDS

Many words have more than one meaning. Clues from the sentence will tell you which meaning is being used. Read each sentence below. Circle the letter of the meaning of the underlined word. Then write a sentence using the other meaning.

1. Have you finished with the first <u>draft</u> of your letter?
   A used for pulling loads
   B a beginning sketch or outline

   _____

2. The math club will <u>recruit</u> four new members.
   A a new member of a club
   B to enlist

   _____

3. Make an <u>outline</u> before you start your report.
   A written notes
   B a line drawing

   _____

4. We needed a wagon to <u>haul</u> the bricks home.
   A a large or heavy load
   B to pull

   _____

5. The river's <u>current</u> was strong.
   A a swift part of a stream
   B part of the present time

   _____

© Harcourt

Vocabulary Power

Name _____

RHYMING WORDS

▶ Use words from the Word Box to complete the sentences below. The word you write should rhyme with the underlined word in the sentence.

fed	tent	fine	rice	mall	sketch	draft

1. I almost <u>laughed</u> when I read my first _____.

2. I'll ask Rover to <u>fetch</u> my _____.

3. We need a truck to <u>haul</u> what we bought at the _____.

4. The teacher said my <u>outline</u> was _____.

5. Wheat is made into <u>bread</u> so that people can be _____.

6. The main <u>event</u> is in the _____.

7. She has a special <u>device</u> for cooking _____.

▶ Now try these.

moth	horse	draw	types	boot	toast	time

8. Everyone <u>saw</u> that he could _____.

9. Did the <u>recruit</u> find his _____?

10. Fabrics have <u>stripes</u> of many _____.

11. The zebra, of <u>course</u>, looks like a _____.

12. It's not hard to <u>rhyme</u> if you take your _____.

13. The holes in the <u>cloth</u> are from the _____.

14. Who ate the <u>most</u> _____?

Vocabulary Power

WORD FAMILIES

▶ **Two words in each group belong in the same word family. Circle the word that does not belong in that word family. Then replace it with another word. The first one is tricky, so it is done for you. (Did you know that *draft* and *draw* both come from the same word family?)**

1. draft   (drama)   draw   _drawing_

2. discover   discourage   uncover   _____

3. replace   place   play   _____

4. value   valueless   valve   _____

5. us   useful   use   _____

6. handy   handkerchief   hamburger   _____

7. seashore   search   seaweed   _____

8. current   currency   rent   _____

9. ant   army   armor   _____

10. enjoyment   engine   enjoy   _____

11. football   footstep   food   _____

12. friendship fruit   fruitcake   _____

13. gentle   gentleman   gemstone   _____

14. grandfather children   grandmother _____

15. cheerful   colorful   coloring   _____

© Harcourt

Name _____

WORD ORIGINS

See how many words from Spanish you already know. Read each pair of words below. Then write the word next to the correct definition.

1. coyote, mustang

a small wild horse _____

a small wolf _____

2. avocado, vanilla

a pear-shaped fruit
with dark skin _____

a flavoring _____

3. Colorado, Florida

a state known for its
red rocks _____
a state known for
its oranges _____

4. mosquito, alligator

a kind of reptile _____

a small insect that bites _____

5. fiesta, guitar

a festival _____
a musical instrument
with strings _____

6. tortilla, taco

a kind of sandwich _____

a flat bread _____

7. piñata, plaza

a marketplace _____
a candy-filled container
hung from the ceiling _____

8. patio, burro

the courtyard of a
Spanish building _____

a donkey _____

Vocabulary Power

Name _____

FIGURATIVE LANGUAGE

Figurative language is using words in a colorful way. Often, the words take on a meaning that is different from the one they usually have.

Example:

Go nuts really means "to get very excited."

▶ **Read each sentence. Then write the meaning of the underlined phrases on the lines.**

1. The colorful flowers were a <u>feast for my eyes</u>.

_____

2. When our team won, we <u>went bananas</u>.

_____

3. The hungry baby <u>howled like a coyote</u>.

_____

4. The land was as <u>flat as a tortilla</u>.

_____

5. The cookies were like a <u>fiesta for my mouth</u>.

_____

▶ **Pick two of the underlined phrases and illustrate them. Label your illustrations on the lines provided.**

Name _____

ANALOGIES

An analogy shows how pairs of words go together.

Example:
   Dog is to bark as cat is to meow.
   (A dog barks; a cat meows.)

Read each analogy below. Figure out how the first two italicized words go together. Then write the word that completes the analogy.

tortilla	leg	asleep	piñata	fire	late
warms	enormous	sleeping	year	plaza	coyote

1. *Fiesta* is to *holiday* as *blaze* is to _____.

2. *Elbow* is to *arm* as *knee* is to _____.

3. *Medicine* is to *cures* as *coat* is to _____.

4. *Merry* is to *miserable* as *small* is to _____.

5. *Cookie* is to *jar* as *candy* is to _____.

6. *Tiger* is to *feline* as _____ is to *canine*.

7. *Bread* is to *sandwich* as _____ is to *taco*.

8. *Restaurant* is to *eating* as _____ is to *shopping*.

9. *Boiling* is to *freezing* as *early* is to _____.

10. *Standing* is to *sitting* as *awake* is to _____.

11. *Day* is to *week* as *month* is to _____.

12. *Kitchen* is to *cooking* as *bedroom* is to _____.

© Harcourt

Vocabulary Power

Name _____

CONNOTATION/DENOTATION

Many words have similar meanings, but similar words can give you different feelings. Would you rather hear someone *sing* or *screech*?

▶ Rate each word in the pair as *more formal* or *less formal*. Write each word under the correct category.

	more formal	less formal
I. company, enterprise	_____	_____
2. dined, ate	_____	_____
3. job, project	_____	_____
4. undertaking, duty	_____	_____
5. dare, venture	_____	_____
6. car, automobile	_____	_____

▶ Rate each word in the pair as *more positive* or *less positive*. Write each word under the correct category.

	more positive	less positive
7. slimy, slippery	_____	_____
8. wet, soggy	_____	_____
9. weird, unusual	_____	_____
10. scrawny, thin	_____	_____
11. tangy, sour	_____	_____
12. house, shack	_____	_____

HOMOGRAPHS AND MULTIPLE-MEANING WORDS

Some words have more than one meaning. Clues from the sentence tell you which meaning is being used. Read each pair of sentences below. Write the letter of the correct meaning next to each sentence.

1. _____ Use the machine to <u>project</u> the slide onto the screen.

   _____ What are you doing for your science <u>project</u>?

   A a piece of work
   B to cause to be seen on a surface

2. _____ Don't lean against the sign <u>post</u>.

   _____ Did you remember to <u>post</u> the letter?

   A a support
   B to mail

3. _____ We started a dog-walking <u>company</u>.

   _____ She enjoyed her friend's <u>company</u>.

   A companionship
   B a business

4. _____ She shed a <u>tear</u> when she fell off her bike.

   _____ Will Mom be able to fix the <u>tear</u> in my shirt?

   A a drop of water from the eye
   B a rip

5. _____ <u>Close</u> the door after yourself.

   _____ We stood <u>close</u> to the fire to stay warm.

   A near
   B to shut

6. _____ I wouldn't <u>venture</u> my life by riding in a car without a seat belt.

   _____ John hopes his business <u>venture</u> will be a success.

   A to risk
   B an investment

7. _____ Sue will <u>wind</u> the thread around the spool.

   _____ Is there enough <u>wind</u> to fly the kite?

   A to wrap around
   B blowing air

Vocabulary Power

Name _____

SYNONYMS

Read each word. Circle the letter of the word that is a synonym for the underlined word. Then write another synonym on the line.

1. project
   A product
   B undertaking
   C proper
   D understand

   _____

2. company
   F cooperate
   G busy
   H compass
   J business

   _____

3. career
   A job
   B careful
   C carefree
   D caretaker

   _____

4. medicine
   F sickness
   G treatment
   H well
   J doctor

   _____

5. venture
   A risk
   B vent
   C rural
   D tranquil

   _____

6. community
   F company
   G toward
   H town
   J command

   _____

7. draft
   A hall
   B haul
   C drama
   D drain

   _____

8. fiesta
   F piñata
   G tortilla
   H work
   J festival

   _____

© Harcourt

Name _____

GREEK AND LATIN ROOTS

▶ The Latin root *vis*, meaning "see," appears in many English words. Study the chart below. Then choose a word to complete each sentence.

Root Word	English Word	Meaning
vis	vision	the sense of sight
vis	visible	able to be seen
vis	visual	having to do with sight
vis	visit	to go or come to see
vis	visor	a brim on the front of a cap
vis	vista	a distant view

1. The lighthouse's beacon was _____ for miles.

2. As a part of our vacation, we planned to _____ a lighthouse.

3. A cap's _____ shades your eyes from the sun.

4. The _____ of the sunset over the ocean spread out before us.

5. A picture is an example of a _____ aid.

6. When you go to the eye doctor, you get your

   _____ checked.

▶ Now complete the chart with two of your own *vis* words.

Root Word	English Word	Meaning
vis		
vis		

Vocabulary Power

Name _____

EXPLORE WORD MEANING

Read and respond to each of the following questions or statements.

1. What are some activities you do where you use your sense of

vision? _____

_____

2. If your vision isn't perfect, what might you wear or do to make it

better? _____

_____

3. What are some visual aids your teacher uses in your classroom?

_____

_____

4. Draw a picture of a cap with a visor.

```
┌─────────────────────────────────────────────────────────┐
│                                                           │
│                                                           │
│                                                           │
│                                                           │
│                                                           │
│                                                           │
└─────────────────────────────────────────────────────────┘
```

5. Draw a vista you might see from a window.

```
┌─────────────────────────────────────────────────────────┐
│                                                           │
│                                                           │
│                                                           │
│                                                           │
│                                                           │
│                                                           │
└─────────────────────────────────────────────────────────┘
```

Name _____

SUFFIXES

The suffix *-ible*, also spelled *-able*, means "capable of being."

Example:
audi, meaning "hear," + *-ible* = *audible*, a word that means "capable of being heard"

Add the suffix *-ible, -able,* to the base words in the chart below to form new words. Write a definition for each new word. The first one is done for you.

Root Word or Base Word	Suffix	New Word	Definition
1. vis	-ible	visible	capable of being seen
2. read	-able		
3. enjoy	-able		
4. break	-able		
5. use	-able		
6. change	-able		
7. love	-able		

Vocabulary Power

Name _____

PREFIXES

Prefixes are added to the beginning of words. They change the meaning of the words. Here are some prefixes and their meanings.

re- again	*over-* too much	*un-* not

▶ **Read each word and the directions. Then choose the correct prefix and add it to the word. Write the new word. The first one is done for you.**

Word	Directions	New Word
1. happy	Change to mean "not happy."	unhappy
2. investigate	Change to mean "to investigate again."	
3. researched	Change to mean "not researched."	
4. examine	Change to mean "to examine again."	
5. build	Change to mean "to build again."	
6. flow	Change to mean "to flow too much"	
7. detected	Change to mean "not detected."	
8. discover	Change to mean "to discover again."	

▶ **Use one of the new words in a sentence.**

_____

_____

Name _____

WORDS IN CONTEXT

▶ **Detective Sharpnose is about to write a mystery novel about his first case. Help him fill in his notes about the case.**

I. Today I'm going to begin to **investigate** a case about _____

_____

2. Before I started, I decided to do some **research** about _____

_____

3. The **research** really helped! I found out _____

_____

4. When I got to the scene, I began to **examine** _____

_____

5. I was excited to **discover** _____

_____

This discovery would help me solve the case!

6. Then I thought I could **detect** a _____

coming from the _____

7. I finally solved the case when _____

_____

▶ **Now write a title for Detective Sharpnose's story.**

_____

_____

Vocabulary Power

CLASSIFY/CATEGORIZE

▶ Write each word from the Word Box in the correct category. Then add a word to each category.

atlas	fairy tale	comic book
encyclopedia	dictionary	mystery story

Books You Use for Research	Books You Read for Fun
_____	_____
_____	_____
_____	_____

▶ Now try these.

mixer	microscope	fork
binoculars	spoon	magnifying glass

Tools You Use to Investigate	Tools You Use in Cooking
_____	_____
_____	_____
_____	_____

© Harcourt

Name _____

RELATED WORDS

The words in the Word Box are related by meaning. Use the Word Box to help you complete the word web about minerals. Fill in the remaining lines with your own words or phrases.

| mines | lodes | geodes | mineralogists | coins |

People Who Work with Minerals

_____
_____
_____
_____

Places Where Minerals Can Be Found

_____
_____
_____
_____

Minerals

Things a Miner Hopes to Find

_____
_____
_____
_____

Uses for Minerals

_____
_____
_____
_____

Vocabulary Power

© Harcourt

Name _____

WORD FAMILIES

Word families are made up of words that have the same root or base word. Read the words below. Circle the letter of the word that does not belong. Then replace it with a word of your own.

1. A miner
   B mineral
   C mineralogist
   D minute

_____

2. F explore
   G examine
   H explorer
   J exploration

_____

3. A secure
   B security
   C second
   D secured

_____

4. F vision
   G violin
   H visor
   J vista

5. A write
   B writer
   C wren
   D wrote

_____

6. F discontent
   G discover
   H discovery
   J discovered

_____

7. A geode
   B geography
   C geographic
   D gentle

_____

8. F cover
   G covering
   H cave
   J covered

_____

Name _____

HOMOPHONES

The words in each homophone pair below are pronounced the same but have different spellings and different meanings. Write the word that matches each clue below.

load–lode	flour–flower	new–knew	sew–sow

1. recently made _____

2. had knowledge of _____

3. to scatter seeds _____

4. to make using needle and thread _____

5. a blossom _____

6. a soft powder used to make bread _____

7. what a person is carrying _____

8. a streak of ore of a metal _____

right–write	minor–miner	herd–heard

9. the opposite of *left* _____

10. to make letters or numbers with a
    pen or pencil _____

11. a group of animals _____

12. listened to _____

13. a person who digs minerals _____

14. not important _____

Vocabulary Power

© Harcourt

Name _____

EXPLORE WORD MEANING

Read and respond to each question or statement.

I. Add **elaboration** to the following statement: It was a very hot day.

_____

_____

2. Write a **description** of your favorite animal, but don't tell what animal you are describing. Have a partner try to guess what animal you described.

_____

_____

3. What kind of **addition** would you like to make to the school playground?

_____

_____

4. Here is a plain cake. Add **embellishment** to it.

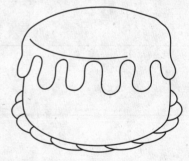

5. The local mall is thinking about getting bigger. What stores should be part of the **expansion**?

_____

_____

© Harcourt

ANALOGIES

An analogy is made up of two pairs of words. Each pair of words is related in the same way.
- For example, the two words in each part of the analogy may be opposites, such as

    Hot is to *cold* as *tall* is to *short.*
- Or, the two words in each part of the analogy may be synonyms, such as

    Beautiful is to *pretty* as *jump* is to *leap.*

Look at each pair of words below. Decide how the words are related. Then complete the analogy. The first one is done for you.

1. (Elaboration, description)
Elaboration is to *description* as *hot* is to _____warm_____.

2. (Sharp, dull)
Sharp is to *dull* as *wet* is to _____.

3. (Embellishment, decoration)
Embellishment is to *decoration* as *photograph* is to _____.

4. (Diary, journal)
Diary is to *journal* as *bake* is to _____.

5. (Child, adult)
Child is to *adult* as *small* is to _____.

6. (Addition, expansion)
Addition is to *expansion* as *describe* is to _____.

7. (Famous, unknown)
Famous is to *unknown* as *dark* is to _____.

8. (Smile, grin)
Smile is to *grin* as *laugh* is to _____.

Vocabulary Power

© Harcourt

Name _____

CONTEXT CLUES

You can often figure out the meaning of an unfamiliar word by looking at the words around it. Read each of the following sentences. Then write a definition of the underlined word. Look at the other words in the sentence for clues.

1. Elaboration, or adding descriptive details, paints a mental picture

   for readers. _____

2. Her funny, lopsided grin was higher on one side than the other.

   _____

3. The new bedroom was an addition to our house.

   _____

4. The cake had yellow stars and pink flowers as embellishments.

   _____

5. His aged hat was worn and faded. _____

6. The amicable shopkeeper was friendly to every customer.

   _____

7. The circus clown wore a ridiculous rubber nose that made all the

   children laugh. _____

8. The cowardly lion was afraid of everything.

   _____

9. After rolling in the dirt, the puppy was grubby. _____

10. Her gracious greeting made me feel welcome. _____

ANALOGIES

In an analogy, two pairs of words are related in the same way.

Example:

Eyes are to *see* as *ears* are to *hear.*

Complete each analogy. The first one is done for you.

1. *Tranquil* is to *blustery* as *fatigue* is to _____zeal_____.

2. *Active* is to *inactive* as *lost* is to _____.

3. *Visor* is to *cap* as *collar* is to _____.

4. *Plate* is to *food* as *cup* is to _____.

5. *Shimmer* is to *star* as *glimmer* is to _____.

6. *Calorie* is to *food* as *watt* is to _____.

7. *Running* is to *track* as *swimming* is to _____.

8. *Mineralogist* is to *minerals* as *herpetologist* is to _____.

9. *Nose* is to *smell* as *eyes* are to _____.

10. *Mittens* are to *hands* as *socks* are to _____.

11. *Fork* is to *eating* as *pencil* is to _____.

12. *Fur* is to *cat* as *scale* is to _____.

13. *Food* is to a *person* as *gasoline* is to a _____.

14. An *instrument* is to a *musician* as a *saw* is to a _____.

15. The *President* is to the *country* as the *mayor* is to the _____.

Vocabulary Power

Name _____

CLASSIFY/CATEGORIZE

Read each group of words below. Circle the letter of the word that does not belong in each group. Then add a category name for each group.

1. **A** rotating
 B talking
 C spinning
 D revolving

_____

2. **F** morning
 G night
 H afternoon
 J winter

_____

3. **A** calorie
 B watt
 C volt
 D thermometer

_____

4. **F** spring
 G summer
 H noon
 J fall

_____

5. **A** sleeping
 B swimming
 C jogging
 D dancing

_____

6. **F** diamond
 G gold
 H silver
 J bracelet

_____

7. **A** ice
 B sun
 C oven
 D fire

_____

8. **F** Washington
 G China
 H Idaho
 J Virginia

_____

9. **A** pony
 B donkey
 C wolf
 D horse

_____

10. **F** flame
 G icicle
 H snow
 J glacier

_____

© Harcourt

Vocabulary Power

ANTONYMS AND SYNONYMS

▶ **Read each word. Find its antonym in the Word Box and write it on the line. Then think of a synonym for the word and write it on the line.**

fatigue	boring	subtraction	lose	real-life	slow

	Antonym	Synonym
1. zeal	_____	_____
2. addition	_____	_____
3. exciting	_____	_____
4. discover	_____	_____
5. fantasy	_____	_____
6. rapid	_____	_____

▶ **Now try these.**

lower	confuse	rough	cry	dislike	impolite

	Antonym	Synonym
7. laugh	_____	_____
8. like	_____	_____
9. raise	_____	_____
10. smooth	_____	_____
11. clarify	_____	_____
12. considerate	_____	_____

Vocabulary Power

PREFIXES

Prefixes are added to the beginning of words. They change the meaning of a word. Here are some prefixes and their meanings.

over- too much	*re-* again	*pre-* before	*in-, im-, il-, ir-* not

When you are adding a prefix that means "not," use *il-* before base words that start with *l*, *ir-* before base words that start with *r*, and *im-* before base words that start with *b*, *m*, or *p*. Use *in-* for base words starting with any other letter.

Read each word and the directions. Then choose the correct prefix and add it to the word. Write the new word.

Word	Directions	New Word
1. visible	Change to mean "not visible."	_____
2. pay	Change to mean "pay too much."	_____
3. arrange	Change to mean "arrange before."	_____
4. possible	Change to mean "not possible."	_____
5. enter	Change to mean "enter again."	_____
6. perfect	Change to mean "not perfect."	_____
7. regular	Change to mean "not regular."	_____
8. active	Change to mean "not active."	_____
9. register	Change to mean "register again."	_____

© Harcourt

ANTONYMS AND SYNONYMS

▶ Read each word. Write its antonym on the line. Then think of a synonym for the word and write it on the next line.

		Antonym	Synonym
1.	visible	_____	_____
2.	strength	_____	_____
3.	easy	_____	_____
4.	push	_____	_____
5.	floating	_____	_____
6.	scamper	_____	_____
7.	wonderful	_____	_____

▶ Now try these.

		Antonym	Synonym
8.	heavy	_____	_____
9.	regular	_____	_____
10.	tear	_____	_____
11.	noisy	_____	_____
12.	pleased	_____	_____
13.	ragged	_____	_____
14.	blustery	_____	_____

WORD FAMILIES

▶ Read the words in the Word Box. Then add them to the correct word web. Use the base word or root word to help you. There are two words in the Word Box you will not use.

visible	regularly	invisible	restore	television
villager	regulate	regulation	visit	irregular

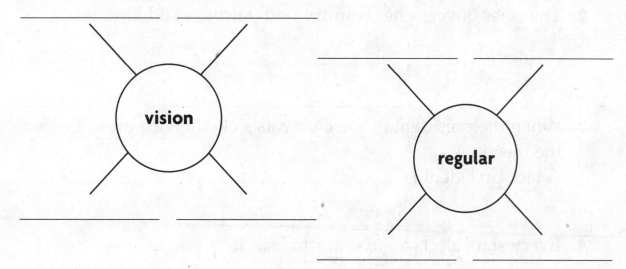

▶ Now try these.

exam	impossible	postage	reexamine	excite
possibility	examination	examined	possibly	impossibility

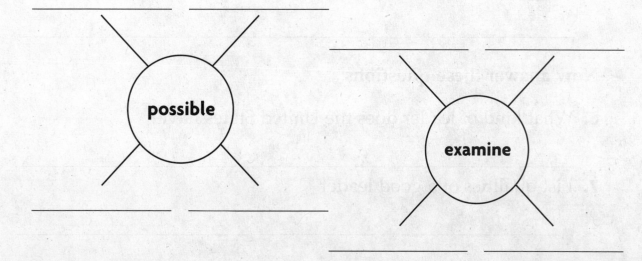

CONTEXT CLUES

▶ **Read each sentence, paying attention to the underlined words. Then write a definition for each underlined word.**

I. The king sent <u>viceroys</u> to the colony to rule in his place.

A viceroy is _____

_____ .

2. The <u>ruler</u> governs her country with fairness and kindness.

A ruler is _____

_____ .

3. When the president of the club was sick, the <u>vice president</u> led the meetings.
A vice president is _____

_____ .

4. Every state elects a <u>governor</u> to lead it.

A governor is _____

_____ .

5. When the sheriff was off duty, the <u>deputy</u> took his place.

A deputy is _____

_____ .

▶ **Now answer these questions.**

6. What kind of leader does the United States have?

_____

7. List qualities of a good leader.

_____

Vocabulary Power

Name _____

COMPARE AND CONTRAST

Read and respond to each question. Then explain your answer.

1. In the United States, who has more responsibility, the <u>Vice president</u> or the <u>President</u>?

_____

2. Who would report to a sheriff, a <u>king</u> or a <u>deputy</u>?

_____

3. Who has more responsibility, a <u>king</u> or a <u>viceroy</u>?

_____

4. Who has more responsibility, the <u>mayor</u> of a city or the <u>governor</u> of a state?

_____

5. Who has more responsibility, the <u>governor</u> of a state or the <u>Vice president</u> of a country?

_____

6. Are a <u>President</u> of a country and a <u>ruler</u> of a country alike?

_____

7. Which would you rather be, a <u>president</u> or a <u>vice president</u>?

_____

8. Are a <u>vice president</u> and a <u>viceroy</u> alike?

_____

© Harcourt

Name _____

MULTIPLE-MEANING WORDS

▶ Many words have more than one meaning. Clues from the sentence will tell you which meaning is being used. Read each sentence below. Circle the letter of the meaning of the underlined word. Then write a sentence using the other meaning.

1. The viceroy made laws for the country.
   A a butterfly
   B a person who rules in place of a king

   _____

2. We measured the string with a ruler.
   A a measuring stick
   B a leader

   _____

3. The balloon rose into the air.
   A a flower
   B to go up

   _____

4. The board is one foot long.
   A a unit of length equal to twelve inches
   B the end of the leg

   _____

5. The doctor gave me medicine to treat my poison ivy.
   A to cure or make better
   B something that gives pleasure

   _____

▶ Read the following sentence. Then write at least two other meanings for the underlined word.

6. The governor of our state is going to run for office.

   _____

Vocabulary Power

Glossary

ad•di•tion [ə•dish′ən] *n.* Something that is added; an annex: **The new library is a helpful** *addition* **to our school.**

ad•ver•tise•ments [ad′vər•tīz′mənts] *n., pl.* Public notices in order to sell something: **The furniture store has** *advertisements* **for tables and chairs on sale.**

ag•ri•cul•tur•al [ag′rə•kul′chər•əl] *adj.* Of, having to do with, or used in farming: **There are still many** *agricultural* **towns in the Midwest.**

an•i•mat•ed film [an′ə•mā′tid film] *n.* A motion picture made up of a series of drawings with moving figures: **Enrico saw an** *animated film* **in which the horse talked.**

an•nu•al [an′yoo•əl] *adj.* Of a plant, living or lasting only a year or a season: **We planted some beautiful** *annual* **flowers in our garden.**

ap•ply [ə•plī′] *v.* To make a formal request: **My father will** *apply* **for the job in Texas.**

ar•chae•ol•o•gy [är′kē•ol′ə•jē] *n.* The study of past times and cultures: **Mallory learned about the Mayan civilization when she studied** *archaeology.*

as•sist [ə•sist′] *v.* To help; aid: **Will you** *assist* **me in lifting this heavy box?**

as•tron•o•my [ə•stron′ə•mē] *n.* The study of stars, planets, and other objects in the sky: **When I go to the science museum, I like to learn about** *astronomy,* **especially Mars.**

ath•let•ic [ath•let′ik] *adj.* Of, for, or having to do with sports and games: **The professional basketball player enjoyed his** *athletic* **career.**

be•liefs [bi•lēfs′] *n., pl.* Things in which one has faith or confidence: **Her family lives by their** *beliefs.*

bi•en•ni•al [bī•en′ē•əl] *adj.* Lasting or living for two years: **It is time to replace those biennial plants.**

bill•board [bil′bôrd′] *n.* A large outdoor panel for notices or

a	add	e	end	o	odd	ōō	pool	oi	oil	<u>th</u>	this
ā	ace	ē	equal	ō	open	u	up	ou	pout	zh	vision
â	care	i	it	ô	order	û	burn	ng	ring		
ä	palm	ī	ice	ŏŏ	took	yōō	fuse	th	thin		

ə = { a in *above* / e in *sicken* / i in *possible* / o in *melon* / u in *circus*

109

advertisements: **The colorful *billboard* by the highway advertised the new amusement park.**

bi•ol•o•gy [bī•ol′ə•jē] *n.* The science of life and of the ways in which living things grow, develop, and reproduce: **You will learn about the parts of a cell when you study *biology*.**

blus•ter•y [blus′tər•ē] *adj.* Noisy; forceful: **During the thunderstorm, it was hard to walk in the *blustery* rain and wind.**

bo•vine [bō′vīn′] *n.* A cow, ox, or other related animal: **The steer is a large *bovine*.**

breez•y [brē′zē] *adj.* Having light, gentle winds: **The *breezy* weather was perfect for flying a kite.**

bright•en [brīt′(ə)n] *v.* 1. To make bright or brighter; illuminate: **We held up our flashlight to *brighten* the dark cave.** 2. To become bright or brighter: **The sky may *brighten* after the storm.**

bul•le•tin [bool′ə•tən] *n.* A short public announcement: **A *bulletin* in today's newspaper announced the sale of a used bicycle.**

C

cal•o•rie [kal′ə•rē] *n.* A unit used to measure the energy-producing value of food: **Even a small piece of candy has more than 1 *calorie*.**

ca•nine [kā′nīn′] *adj.* Belonging to a group of animals that includes dogs, foxes, and wolves: **Much has been written about Native Americans' respect for their *canine* neighbors, wolves.**

car•bo•hy•drate [kär′bō•hī′drāt′] *n.* Any of a large group of compounds, such as sugars and starches, made up of carbon, hydrogen, and oxygen: **A potato is a *carbohydrate*.**

ca•reer [kə•rir′] *n.* A person's lifework or profession: **José always knew that teaching was the *career* for him.**

car•pen•ter [kär′pən•tər] *n.* A person who makes or repairs things, often using wood: **Dad hired a *carpenter* to build a new bookcase.**

car•toon [kär•toon′] *n.* A motion picture made by photographing a series of slightly different drawings so that the figures seem to move:

We laughed when we watched the *cartoon* about a talking dog.

cav•i•ty [kav′ə•tē] *n.* A small hole in a tooth, caused by decay: **I hope the dentist doesn't find a *cavity* in my tooth when I go for a checkup.**

Cel•si•us [sel′sē•əs] *adj.* Of, having to do with, or according to the temperature scale with 0 degrees at the freezing point of water and 100 degrees at its boiling point: **The thermometer showed a temperature of 10 degrees *Celsius*.**

cer•e•mo•nies [ser′ə•mō′nēs] *n., pl.* Any formal acts or series of actions performed in a definite, set manner: **His family observes religious *ceremonies* throughout the year.**

chasm [kaz′əm] *n.* A deep crack or gorge in the surface of the earth: **The hikers stayed away from the edge of the *chasm*.**

cin•e•ma [sin′ə•mə] *n.* A motion picture theater: **We saw the new movie at the *cinema*.**

clar•i•fy [klar′ə•fī] *v.* To make something more understandable: **I asked her to *clarify* the directions to her house.**

col•lab•o•rate [kə•lab′ə•rāt′] *v.* To work together, as on literary or scientific efforts: **They decided to *collaborate* on the book of short stories.**

com•mu•ni•ty [kə•myo͞o′nə•tē] *n.* 1. A group of people who live in the same place: **Our *community* voted to support this neighborhood garden.** 2. A place or area where people live: **This is a very safe *community*.**

com•pa•ny [kum′pə•nē] *n.* 1. A business firm or organization: **She works for a telephone *company*.** 2. Companionship: **I enjoy my friend's *company*.**

con•fi•dence [kon′fə•dəns] *n.* Firm belief or trust: **Andy has a lot of *confidence* in his singing ability.**

co•op•er•ate [kō•op′ə•rāt′] *v.* To work with others for a common purpose: **When we *cooperate*, our work gets done faster and we have more free time.**

a add	e end	o odd	o͞o pool	oi oil	th this	ə =	a in *above*
ā ace	ē equal	ō open	u up	ou pout	zh vision		e in *sicken*
â care	i it	ô order	û burn	ng ring			i in *possible*
ä palm	ī ice	o͝o took	yo͞o fuse	th thin			o in *melon*
							u in *circus*

coy•o•te [kī•ō′tē] *n.* An animal of the western prairies of North America that is smaller than but related to the wolf: **We could hear a *coyote* howling somewhere across the prairie.**

cra•ter [krā′tər] *n.* A bowl-shaped hollow in the ground: **There was a deep *crater* where a meteorite hit many years ago.**

cur•rent [kûr′ənt] *n.* That part of any body of water or air that flows more or less in a definite direction: **They worked hard to paddle the canoe against the river's *current*.**

cus•toms [kus′təmz] *n., pl.* Things that have become accepted practices by many people: **Preparing a feast for Thanksgiving is one of the *customs* that many Americans follow.**

D

de•cid•u•ous [di•sij′o͞o•əs] *adj.* Shedding leaves every year: **We have to rake the leaves from our *deciduous* trees every fall.**

de•gree [di•grē′] *n.* A unit for measuring temperature: **It may snow if the temperature drops**

one more *degree*.

de•moc•ra•cy [di•mok′rə•sē] *n.* A form of government in which the people rule: **Each person has certain rights in a *democracy*.**

dep•u•ty [dep′yə•tē] *n.* A person given the power to do another's job or act in another's place: **The sheriff's *deputy* gave the man a ticket for speeding.**

de•scrip•tion [di•skrip′shən] *n.* 1. The act of describing: **He used *description* to tell about the sunset.** 2. An account given in words: **Tamika gave a *description* of the man she had seen.**

de•tect [di•tekt′] *v.* To discover, especially something hidden or hard to see: **It took her a few minutes to *detect* the small crack in the window.**

de•vice [di•vīs′] *n.* An instrument or tool: **A drill is a *device* for making holes.**

dig•ni•ty [dig′nə•tē] *n.* Proper pride in one's worth or position: **The governor behaves with great *dignity*.**

dis•cov•er [dis•kuv′ər] *v.* To learn or find out, especially for the first time: **I was surprised to *discover* that she had been a teacher for thirty years.**

dol·drums [dōl′drəmz] *n.* The parts of the ocean that are near the equator and have little or no wind much of the time: **The ship sailed through the *doldrums* as it neared the equator.**

draft [draft] *adj.* Used for pulling heavy loads: **Trucks and machines now do the work that *draft* horses did years ago.**

E

e·col·o·gy [i·kol′ə·jē] *n.* The relationship of plants and animals to each other and their surroundings: **In the study of *ecology*, we learn how living things interact.**

e·lab·o·ra·tion [i·lab′ə·rā′shən] *n.* The further development of; the addition of details: **Much of her story is an *elaboration* about Cinderella at the ball.**

e·lec·tri·cian [i·lek′trish′ən] *n.* A person who designs, installs, operates, or repairs electrical equipment or machinery: **The *electrician* fixed the wiring for our new lights.**

em·bel·lish·ment [im·bel′ish·mənt] *n.* Something added for a pleasing effect; decoration: **The flowers made out of icing are a nice *embellishment* for the cake.**

en·er·gy [en′ər·jē] *n.* The ability to do work or give power; usable electric or heat power: **The electric company supplies *energy* to our homes for lights, cooking, and watching TV.**

en·list [in·list′] *v.* To join an activity or cause: **I would like to *enlist* to help with the neighborhood cleanup project.**

en·roll [in·rōl′] *v.* To put one's name on a list, as for membership; register: **Brianna will have to *enroll* at a new school after she moves to a different city.**

en·ter·prise [en′tər·prīz′] *n.* An activity set up to earn money: **Rich was excited about his new *enterprise* and put up a sign that said "Lemonade Stand: Open for Business."**

a	add	e	end	o	odd	o͞o	pool	oi	oil	th	this		*a* in *above*
ā	ace	ē	equal	ō	open	u	up	ou	pout	zh	vision		*e* in *sicken*
â	care	i	it	ô	order	û	burn	ng	ring			ə =	*i* in *possible*
ä	palm	ī	ice	o͝o	took	yo͞o	fuse	th	thin				*o* in *melon*
													u in *circus*

en·ter·tain·ment [en′tər·tān′mənt] *n.* The act of holding the attention and giving enjoyment: **I would like *entertainment* to be my lifework, so I may take acting lessons.**

ep·i·sode [ep′ə·sōd′] *n.* Any incident or event that is part of something continuous, as a story or a person's life: **I just watched the final *episode* of that television program.**

e·quine [ē′kwīn′] *adj.* Of, related to, or like a horse: **The donkey is an *equine* animal.**

ev·er·green [ev′ər·grēn′] *adj.* Having leaves that stay green throughout the year: **In Florida, the *evergreen* trees look beautiful all year.**

ex·am·ine [ig·zam′in] *v.* To look at with care and attention: **The doctor had to *examine* my broken arm before he put the cast on it.**

ex·pan·sion [ik·span′shən] *n.* Something, such as a part or a surface, that results from an enlargement: **The *expansion* of our gym includes new bleachers.**

ex·pe·ri·ence [ik·spir′ē·əns] *n.* Something one has gone through: Jamal's summer camp *experience* was a happy one because he made new friends and learned new games.

ex·plain [ik·splān′] *v.* To make plain or understandable: **He asked the teacher to *explain* how to write a paragraph.**

Fahr·en·heit [far′ən·hīt′] *adj.* Of, having to do with, or according to the temperature scale with 32 degrees at the freezing point and 212 degrees at its boiling point: **When the forecaster says it is 80 degrees *Fahrenheit*, I know it is warm outside.**

fan·ta·sy [fan′tə·sē] *n.* A story about things and people that could not be real: **When I read a book about a boy who was made from a computer, I knew it was a *fantasy*.**

fa·tigue [fə·tēg′] *n.* A tired condition resulting from hard work, effort, or strain: **I suffered *fatigue* after my baseball team played a doubleheader.**

fed·er·al [fed′ər·əl] *adj.* Having to do with the central government of the United States: **City laws, state**

laws, and *federal* laws are all necessary to make the country run.

fe·line [fē′līn′] *n.* An animal of the cat family: **The cougar is a very fast *feline*.**

fi·es·ta [fē·es′tə] *n.* A celebration: **Cinco de Mayo is a well-known Mexican *fiesta*.**

G

gal·ax·y [gal′ək·sē] *n.* A large system of stars and other celestial bodies: **Earth is in the Milky Way *galaxy*.**

ge·ode [jē′ōd′] *n.* A small, hollow stone whose inside wall is lined with crystals: **He cut open the *geode* and showed us how the inside sparkled.**

glim·mer·ing [glim′ər·ing] *adj.* Shining with a faint, unsteady light: **The room was lit by the *glimmering* candles on the cake.**

glis·ten·ing [glis′(ə)n·ing] *adj.* Shining or sparkling, as with reflected light: **On a sunny day, you may find many *glistening* stones at the beach.**

gorge [gôrj] 1. *n.* A narrow, very deep ravine; canyon: **When we looked down, we could see a river flowing at the bottom of the *gorge*.** 2. *v.* To stuff with food: **Sometimes animals will *gorge* themselves if they are very hungry.**

gov·ern·ment [guv′ər(n)·mənt] *n.* The organization through which control or administration of the activities of a nation, state, city, or the like, take place: **In some systems of *government*, only one ruler has power.**

gov·er·nor [guv′ər·nər] *n.* The elected chief executive of a state of the United States: **Our state will elect a new *governor* next year.**

gust·y [gus′tē] *adj.* Having a strong rush of wind: **I could hardly keep my umbrella from blowing away in the *gusty* wind.**

H

haugh·ty [hô′tē] *adj.* Satisfied with oneself and scornful of others; arrogant: **The *haughty* general refused to listen to the concerns of his troops.**

a add	e end	o odd	o͞o pool	oi oil	th this	a in *above*
ā ace	ē equal	ō open	u up	ou pout	zh vision	e in *sicken*
â care	i it	ô order	û burn	ng ring		ə = i in *possible*
ä palm	ī ice	o͝o took	y͞o͞o fuse	th thin		o in *melon*
						u in *circus*

haul [hôl] *v.* To move or carry, as in a truck: **We had to *haul* the wood to the bonfire in our pickup truck.**

her·pe·tol·o·gy [hûr′pə·tol′ə·jē] *n.* The science that studies reptiles and amphibians: **She had to study snakes and alligators in her class on *herpetology*.**

hol·low [hol′ō] 1. *adj.* Empty on the inside: **The *hollow* drum made a low sound when she struck it.** 2. *n.* An empty space in something; hole: **The rabbit hopped into the *hollow* to hide.**

I

il·lu·mi·nate [i·lōō′mə·nāt′] *v.* To light up: **Bright stars *illuminate* the night sky.**

im·ag·i·nar·y [i·maj′ə·ner′ē] *adj.* Existing only in the mind; unreal: **Sometimes it's fun to read about an *imaginary* place.**

im·pos·si·ble [im·pos′ə·bəl] *adj.* Not capable of being, being done, or taking place: **It will be *impossible* to catch the bus.**

in·ci·dent [in′sə·dənt] *n.* An event, often one of little importance: **The *incident* on the playground was not serious.**

in·jec·tion [in·jek′shən] *n.* A substance that is injected, especially a liquid solution of medicine: **This *injection* will protect you from getting the measles.**

in·stru·ment [in′strə·mənt] *n.* A tool for making music: **Maria knows how to play the guitar, but that *instrument* is not used in her school band.**

in·ves·ti·gate [in·ves′tə·gāt′] *v.* To study thoroughly to find out details: **We can *investigate* other planets by looking through telescopes.**

in·vis·i·ble [in·viz′ə·bəl] *adj.* Not able to be seen: **Animals whose colors blend in with their environment are almost *invisible*.**

ir·reg·u·lar [i·reg′yə·lər] *adj.* Not agreeing with usual standards, established patterns, or traditional rules: **His *irregular* behavior caught the attention of the teachers.**

le·gal [lē′gəl] *adj.* Of or having to do with law: **The *legal* system in this country has many levels.**

light•en [līt′(ə)n] *v.* 1. To make light or bright: **The art teacher instructed us to *lighten* the background of our pictures.** 2. To make less heavy: **You can *lighten* your backpack by putting some of your books in my bag.**

lode [lōd] *n.* A vein or layer of metal ore in rock: **Geologists have found a *lode* of silver.**

lo•go [lō′gō] *n.* An identifying symbol often used in advertising: **We use our company's *logo* on all of our letters.**

ma•chin•ist [mə•shē′nist] *n.* A person who is skilled in using machine tools: **The *machinist* made a special part at the factory.**

ma•son [mā′sən] *n.* A person who is skilled in building with materials such as stone, brick, or concrete: **The *mason* added water to the concrete mix.**

med•i•cal [med′i•kəl] *adj.* Of or having to do with medicine: **The nurse gave me a *medical* report to take to my doctor.**

med•i•cine [med′ə•sən] *n.* Any substance used in treating disease, in healing, or in relieving pain: **The doctor prescribed *medicine* for the pain.**

mer•cu•ry [mûr′kyə•rē] *n.* A heavy, poisonous, silver-white metallic element that is liquid and volatile at ordinary temperatures. Pure mercury is used in thermometers and barometers. **The *mercury* in a thermometer rises when the temperature goes up.**

me•te•or [mē′tē•ər] *n.* A small fragment of matter from outer space that is heated white-hot by friction with the earth's atmosphere and appears briefly as a streak of light: **When we sat outside last night, we saw a *meteor*.**

min•er [mīn′ər] *n.* A person who works at digging minerals from the earth: **The *miner* wore a hard hat to protect himself from falling rocks.**

min•er•al [min′ər•əl] *n.* A natural material that does not come from a plant or an animal: **A diamond is a *mineral* with high value.**

a add	e end	o odd	o͞o pool	oi oil	t͟h this	*a* in *above*
ā ace	ē equal	ō open	u up	ou pout	zh vision	*e* in *sicken*
â care	i it	ô order	û burn	ng ring		ə = *i* in *possible*
ä palm	ī ice	o͝o took	yo͞o fuse	th thin		*o* in *melon*
						u in *circus*

min·er·al·o·gist [min′ə·rol′ə·jist] *n.* A person who scientifically studies minerals: **The *mineralogist* used a microscope to look closely at the rock.**

mon·ar·chy [mon′ər·kē] *n.* Government by a ruler such as a king or a queen: **The government in that tiny kingdom is a *monarchy*.**

mo·tion pic·ture [mō′shən pik′chər] *n.* A series of pictures flashed on a screen in rapid succession, making things in the pictures seem to move: **A *motion picture* may have special effects that seem to happen but are imaginary.**

mov·ie [mōō′vē] *n.* A motion picture: **Last night we went to see a *movie*.**

nat·u·ral [nach′ər·əl] *adj.* Produced by or existing in nature; not artificial: **We were fascinated by the *natural* rock formations we saw on the hike.**

neigh·bor·hood [nā′bər·hŏŏd′] *n.* A small area or section of a city or town, often having a special quality

or character: **The *neighborhood* near the docks is the oldest in the city.**

nu·tri·ent [n(y)ōō′trē·ənt] *n.* Something in food that helps people, animals, and plants stay healthy: **Vitamin D, a *nutrient* found in milk, helps teeth stay strong.**

nu·tri·tion·ist [n(y)ōō·trish′ən·ist] *n.* A person who studies food and nourishment: **Kelly works as a *nutritionist* at the hospital.**

nu·tri·tious [n(y)ōō·trish′əs] *adj.* Giving nourishment; nourishing: **Orange juice is a *nutritious* beverage because it contains vitamin C.**

O

out·line [out′līn′] *n.* A written plan of the most important points, as of a speech or a story: **Megan used her notes to write an *outline* for her research report.**

P

part·ner [pärt′nər] *n.* A person who performs an activity with another or others: **You must have a *partner* in order to compete in the three-legged race.**

per•cus•sion [pər•kush′ən] *adj.* Having a tone produced by striking or hitting, as a drum: **My favorite *percussion* instrument is the cymbal.**

per•en•ni•al [pə•ren′ē•əl] *adj.* Of a plant, living or lasting for more than two years or seasons: **I look forward to the *perennial* flowers in our garden blooming every year.**

pi•ña•ta [pēn•yä′tə] *n.* A decorated, candy-filled container that is hung from the ceiling at traditional Latin American celebrations. Blindfolded children try to break it open with a stick. **I hope I can get some candy when the *piñata* is broken!**

plan•et [plan′it] *n.* Any of the relatively large, nonglowing bodies that move in orbits around the sun or another star: **Mercury is the *planet* that is closest to the sun.**

pla•za [plä′zə] *n.* An open square or marketplace in a town or city: **We bought fresh vegetables at a produce stand in the *plaza*.**

plumb•er [plum′ər] *n.* A person whose business is installing or repairing water pipes: **A *plumber* came to fix the leak in our sink.**

pop•u•la•tion [pop′yə•lā′shən] *n.* The total number of people living in a place, such as a country or city: **The *population* of our city is 100,752.**

por•cine [pôr′sīn] *adj.* Of or similar to swine or pigs: **The *porcine* dog ate during most of the day.**

pos•si•ble [pos′ə•bəl] *adj.* Having a chance of happening: **It is *possible* that we will see someone we know at the park.**

prac•tic•es [prak′tis•əz] *n., pl.* A person's customary or usual actions; habits: **It is one of my *practices* to take a walk every evening.**

pre•cau•tion [pri•kô′shən] *n.* Care taken to avoid possible harm or danger: **As a *precaution* against getting burned, never touch a hot pan.**

pre•heat [prē•hēt′] *v.* To heat something before it is used: **We must *preheat* the oven to 400 degrees Fahrenheit before baking the brownies.**

a	add	e	end	o	odd	o͞o	pool	oi	oil	th	this		*a* in *above*
ā	ace	ē	equal	ō	open	u	up	ou	pout	zh	vision		*e* in *sicken*
â	care	i	it	ô	order	û	burn	ng	ring			ə =	*i* in *possible*
ä	palm	ī	ice	o͝o	took	yo͞o	fuse	th	thin				*o* in *melon*
													u in *circus*

pre·his·tor·ic [prē′his·tôr′ik] *adj.* Of or belonging to the time before written history: **Most** *prehistoric* **animals are now extinct.**

pre·judge [prē·juj′] *v.* To judge beforehand, without proper knowledge: **It is not good to** *prejudge* **others based on how they look.**

pre·pay [prē·pā′] *v.* To pay or pay for in advance: **We had to** *prepay* **for our tickets to the baseball game.**

pre·tend [pri·tend′] *v.* To make believe: **Kim and I like to** *pretend* **we are famous.**

proj·ect [*n.* proj′ekt], **pro·ject** [*v.* prə·jekt′] 1. *n.* A problem, task, or piece of work: **Tyra presented her science** *project* **to the class.** 2. *v.* To cause (an image or shadow) to be seen on a surface: **He used a slide projector to** *project* **the pictures onto the screen.**

pro·tein [prō′tēn′] *n.* Any of a large group of complex organic compounds containing nitrogen; a necessary part of our diet: **Fish is a good source of** *protein.*

R

re·cruit [ri·kro͞ot′] 1. *v.* To cause to join a group or organization: **We should** *recruit* **Tanya to help with our group project.** 2. *n.* A new member of a group or organization: **The army** *recruit* **had not yet learned all the rules.**

reg·is·ter [rej′is·tər] *v.* To enter a name in an official list: **Sue will have to** *register* **to vote if she wants to vote in the next election.**

reg·u·lar [reg′yə·lər] *adj.* Usual; always occurring at the same time: **Our** *regular* **practice was rescheduled because of the rain.**

rem·e·dy [rem′ə·dē] *n.* Something that cures, relieves, or corrects: **Aspirin is one** *remedy* **for headaches.**

re·pub·lic [ri·pub′lik] *n.* A form of government in which elected officials represent the people: **The United States is a** *republic.*

re·quest [ri·kwest′] *v.* To ask for: **We can** *request* **an appointment with the school counselor.**

re·search [rē′sûrch′] *v.* To investigate and study carefully:

Did you *research* several topics before choosing one for your report?

rul•er [roō′lər] *n.* A person who governs with supreme authority: **The prince is the *ruler* of that part of the nation.**

ru•ral [roōr′əl] *adj.* Relating to a country area: **Their farm is outside the city in a *rural* part of the county.**

rus•tic [rus′tik] *adj.* Of or having to do with the country rather than a city: **My grandparents grew up in a *rustic* fishing village.**

se•cure [si•kyoōr′] *adj.* Free from fear or worry: **She is *secure* in knowing that her parents and teachers care for her.**

set•tle•ment [set′(ə)l•mənt] *n.* An area newly settled by people: **A large city often begins as a small *settlement*.**

shim•mer•ing [shim′ər•ing] *adj.* Shining with a faint, unsteady light: **In the moonlight, you can see the *shimmering* ripples on the lake.**

sit•u•a•tion [sich′oō•wā′shən] *n.* A condition or state of affairs caused by a combination of circumstances: **The hikers were in a bad *situation*, with no food or shelter.**

slo•gan [slō′gən] *n.* A phrase or motto used in advertising or campaigning to draw attention: **The candidate for class president printed her *slogan* on each poster.**

so•cial [sō′shəl] *adj.* Liking or tending to live together in communities: **Elephants are *social* animals.**

so•lar sys•tem [sō′lər sis′təm] *n.* The sun, the planets, and other celestial bodies that revolve around the sun: **Our *solar system* has nine planets.**

spar•kling [spär′kling] *adj.* Lively: **Her *sparkling* eyes danced with joy when she saw her birthday presents.**

tale [tāl] *n.* A story: **That novel is a *tale* about the Iditarod dogsled race in Alaska.**

a	add	e	end	o	odd	ōō	pool	oi	oil	th	this		a in *above*
ā	ace	ē	equal	ō	open	u	up	ou	pout	zh	vision		e in *sicken*
â	care	i	it	ô	order	û	burn	ng	ring			ə =	i in *possible*
ä	palm	ī	ice	oō	took	yoō	fuse	th	thin				o in *melon*
													u in *circus*

team•work [tēm′wûrk′] *n.* United effort: **We need *teamwork* to win this match.**

tech•nol•o•gy [tek•nol′ə•jē] *n.* The application of science and industrial skills to practical uses: **Many people believe that as *technology* gets better, our quality of life will improve.**

tem•per•a•ture [tem′prə•chər] *n.* The degree of heat or cold in a body or thing, as measured on some definite scale: **The *temperature* of the room is rising.**

tor•til•la [tôr•tē′yä] *n.* A round, flat Mexican bread made of cornmeal: **I ate a *tortilla* at the Mexican restaurant.**

tra•di•tions [trə•dish′ənz] *n., pl.* Customs that are passed on from parents to children: **Barbecues and fireworks are some *traditions* for the Fourth of July.**

tran•quil [trang′kwil] *adj.* Calm, peaceful: **The day was *tranquil* and the birds were singing.**

treat•ment [trēt′mənt] *n.* An action taken to help make something better: **The doctor told me to apply a cream as a *treatment* for poison oak.**

twin•kling [twing′kling] *n.* Sparkling or shining: **The *twinkling* of the stars made the night sky beautiful.**

un•der•tak•ing [un′dər•tā′king] *n.* Something one tries to do: **Erin's father wanted to paint the whole house himself, but that enormous *undertaking* was too much for one person.**

un•de•vel•oped [un′di•vel′əpt] *adj.* Not yet at full growth: **My house is in an *undeveloped* area, but new roads are being built there.**

u•ten•sil [yoo•ten′səl] *n.* A tool or piece of equipment used to do something: **A fork is an eating *utensil*.**

vac•cine [vak•sēn′] *n.* Medicine that puts weak or dead germs into the body to prevent disease: **My mother and father got the flu *vaccine*.**

vain [vān] *adj.* Overly self-admiring; showing too much pride in oneself: **He was so *vain* that he talked about no one but himself.**

ven•ture [ven′chər] *n.* A plan to do something involving some risk: **The new business is a *venture* that might not succeed.**

vice pres•i•dent [vīs prez′ə•dənt] *n.* The person ranked below a president: **When we choose a new president, we will also choose a new *vice president*.**

vice•roy [vīs′roy′] *n.* A ruler of a country, a state, a city, or a township: **The court of the *viceroy* was made up of people who helped him make laws.**

vis•i•ble [viz′ə•bəl] *adj.* Able to be seen: **Amy's white jacket was *visible* way down the street.**

vi•sion [vizh′ən] *n.* The ability to see: **The doctor said my *vision* was excellent.**

vi•sor [vī′zər] *n.* Something that gives shade for the eyes, such as part of a cap: **When I play tennis, the *visor* of my cap helps keep the sunlight out of my eyes.**

vis•ta [vis′tə] *n.* A view: **The room on the top floor of the building provided a wonderful *vista* of the city.**

vis•u•al [vizh′o͞o•əl] *adj.* Having to do with the sense of sight: **A picture book is more *visual* than a dictionary.**

watt [wot] *n.* A unit of electric power or energy: **The tiny light bulb that she invented uses just one *watt* of power.**

wood•wind [wo͝od′wind′] *n.* Any of a group of musical wind instruments, such as a clarinet or a flute: **He plays the saxophone, a *woodwind*, in the band.**

yarn [yärn] *n.* A story, usually long and exaggerated, that is made up: **Mike's uncle said he used to spin a *yarn* when he told his children a bedtime story.**

zeal [zēl] *n.* Great interest and enthusiasm: **Leon displayed *zeal* for his topic when he gave a speech about adopting a pet.**

a add	e end	o odd	o͞o pool	oi oil	t̶h̶ this	a in *above*
â ace	ē equal	ō open	u up	ou pout	zh vision	e in *sicken*
â care	i it	ô order	û burn	ng ring	ə =	i in *possible*
ä palm	ī ice	o͝o took	yo͞o fuse	th thin		o in *melon*
						u in *circus*

My Own Word List